Engraved portrait of Thomas Gray, after a painting by John Giles Eckhardt. It was used as a frontispiece in Volume II of his *Works*. Image taken from *Instructions by Thomas Grey to his Publisher*.

Titles in the *Shearsman Classics* series:

Forthcoming

Thomas Gray

The English Poems

Shearsman Books

Published in the United Kingdom in 2014 by
Shearsman Books Ltd
50 Westons Hill Drive
Emersons Green
BRISTOL
BS16 7DF

www.shearsman.com

Shearsman Classics Vol. 19
ISBN 978-1-84861-357-7

Contents

INTRODUCTION

Thomas Gray (1716–1771) is a poet with a strange reputation. At least one of his poems is considered to be an indispensable classic; others provide quotable lines or phrases that live on two and a half centuries later, often without the users realising that Gray was their original author. His *oeuvre* is slim, and he ceased writing poetry long before his death. He was offered the Laureateship upon the death of the long-forgotten Colley Cibber, but declined the post. Some of his work is distinctly *dusty* and worthy of consignment to the history books; several poems however show astonishing verve and virtuosity, and it is clear that he was indeed something of a prodigy. He gave up writing verse seriously, perhaps because he too sensed that the fire had burned down to little more than embers. So what is left? Enough work, I would suggest, to support the slender reputation that still clings to his name, but—it must be admitted—he never again managed to hit the heights of the 'Elegy', by any standards an astonishing piece of work. Gray's early reputation was founded upon this poem; it was published early, on its own, and ran though eleven editions, including an illustrated edition and a Latin translation by other hands. In this book you will find all of his verse in English—he also wrote in Greek and Latin, but translations of these do not much help the modern reader and they have thus been excluded.

Thomas Gray was born in London, in a house on Cornhill in the City of London, on 26 December 1716. His grandfather had been a successful merchant, but his father took up work as a money-scrivener—a loan-broker in modern parlance—and was not too successful. In fact, when his father died, the family was left in somewhat straitened circumstances. The younger Gray was however educated at Eton, where he was to meet young men who were to be important to him in later life, such as Richard West—subject of an Epitaph by Gray, and son of the Lord Chancellor of Ireland—and Horace Walpole—author of *The*

Castle of Otranto and creator of the magnificent mock-Gothic house, Strawberry Hill—who was later to publish some of Gray's work. In 1734 Gray went up to Cambridge, and maintained a lengthy correspondence with West who was at Christ Church, Oxford. Both men decided that they would take up the Law; West entered the Inner Temple in 1738 and Gray intended to do likewise, but decided instead to accept Walpole's invitation to accompany him on his Grand Tour. Gray's pleasure at being involved in this enterprise was tempered by a significant falling-out between the young men, which occasioned the poet's return to England, and a lengthy estrangement between the two men. Gray's father passed away only shortly after his return from the Continent. Gray then returned to Cambridge and studied for a degree in Civil Law.

It is hard to date Gray's real beginnings as a poet, notwithstanding the existence of at least one poem from 1734, but he certainly wrote his Epitaph for Gray in 1742, and appears to have written the 'Ode on the Spring' before West's death, while visiting his mother at Stoke Poges. The 'Ode on a Distant Prospect of Eton College' dates from 1742, as does the 'Hymn to Adversity'. The 'Ode on the Death of a Favourite Cat' dates from 1747, the poor cat being Walpole's.

Gray continued to live in Cambridge for the rest of his days, apart from a brief sojourn in London's Southampton Row, near the new British Museum, where he consulted a number of old volumes while trying to write an abortive *History of English Poetry.* While his mother lived, he was a regular visitor to Stoke Poges, and the churchyard there is the subject of his most famous poem—composed *ca.* 1750—as well as the burial place of both the poet and his mother.

He led the life of a gentleman scholar in Cambridge and, through the good offices of the Duke of Grafton in 1768, was made King's Professor of Modern History at the University, with an attendant income of £400 p.a.—a not inconsiderable sum. Three years later he fell ill while in London, suffered an attack of "gout of the stomach" after his return to his college, and passed away a few days later at the age of 54.

THE TEXT

Given that Gray's work is easily available online in modernised form, and is anthologised far and wide in various guises, I have decided in this edition to offer, as far I am able, the original versions, and even to mimic the 18th-century presentation, although that might be regarded in some quarters as an affectation. The source for the first section is the London edition of *Poems by Mr Gray* (1768); reference has also been made to the Glasgow edition of the same year—although this slightly postdates the London edition, and the London edition has therefore been given preference. Subsequent texts follow the first-publication versions. Poems in manuscript have come from a number of sources, some of them photo-reproductions of the manuscripts and others from transcriptions by previous editors. This volume makes no pretence of being a scholarly edition with intensively-researched textual presentation. It does however attempt to be as accurate as possible within its limitations.

Tony Frazer

BIBLIOGRAPHY

Books

An Ode on a Distant Prospect of Eton College (London: Printed for R. Dodsley and sold by M. Cooper, 1747).

An Elegy Wrote in a Country Church Yard (London: Printed for R. Dodsley and sold by M. Cooper, 1751).

Designs by Mr. R. Bentley, for Six Poems by Mr. T. Gray (London: Printed for R. Dodsley, 1753).

Odes, by Mr. Gray (London: Printed at Strawberry-Hill, for R. and J. Dodsley, 1757).

Poems by Mr. Gray (London: Printed for J. Dodsley, 1768).

The Poems of Mr. Gray: To Which Are Prefixed Memoirs of His Life and Writings by W. Mason, M.A. (York: Printed by A. Ward; and sold by J. Dodsley, London; and J. Todd, York, 1775).

The Works of Thomas Gray, in Prose and Verse, 4 volumes, edited by Edmund Gosse (London: Macmillan, 1884).

Gray's English Poems, Original, and Translated from the Norse and Welsh, edited by D. C. Tovey (Cambridge: University Press, 1898).

Gray and Collins: Poetical Works, ed. Austen Lane Poole (Oxford: Oxford University Press, 1919; 3rd edn, 1937).

The Complete Poems of Thomas Gray: English, Latin and Greek, edited by H. W. Starr and J. R. Hendrickson (Oxford: Clarendon Press, 1966).

The Thomas Gray Archive, ed. Alexander Huber. <http://www.thomasgray.org>

Other

Robert Dodsley, ed., *A Collection of Poems: By Several Hands*, Vol. 2, includes Gray's poems 'Ode on the Spring', 'Ode on the Death of a Favourite Cat', and 'Ode on a Distant Prospect of Eton College' (London: Printed for R. Dodsley, 1748).

Letters

The Correspondence of Thomas Gray, 3 vols, edited by Paget Toynbee and Leonard Whibley (Oxford: Clarendon Press, 1935; reprinted, with additions and corrections by Herbert W. Starr, Oxford: Clarendon Press, 1971).

Manuscripts

A commonplace book, in three volumes, at Pembroke College, Cambridge, contains autograph manuscripts of many of Gray's poems, as well as transcripts of other poems by Gray made by William Mason after the author's death. An early version of the 'Elegy' is at Eton College and is printed in this volume.

1716 Thomas Gray born 26 December in Cornhill, London, where his mother, Dorothy (1685-1753, *née* Antrobus), ran a milliner's shop with her sister, Mary. His father, Philip Gray (1676-1741), was a money scrivener by profession.
Thomas was the only child to survive, out of twelve.

1725 Gray sent to Eton, under the care of his uncle, Robert Antrobus, who was assistant master at the college. He made lifelong friendships with Richard West (1716-42), Horace Walpole (1717-97), and Thomas Ashton (1715-1775).

1734 Entered as pensioner at Peterhouse, Cambridge; fully admitted later in the year.
Met Thomas Wharton, a pensioner at Pembroke College.
8 Dec. Gray wrote his first surviving English poem, 'Lines Spoken by John Dennis at the Devil Tavern', which he sent to Walpole.

1735 Joined in Cambridge by his friend Horace Walpole, who entered King's College.
May West entered Christ Church, Oxford.
Nov. Gray admitted to the Inner Temple.

1736 *12 Feb.* Inherited the small property of his paternal aunt, Sarah Gray.
May Gray's 'Hymeneal' on the marriage of the Prince of Wales published in the Cambridge *Gratulatio*, a celebratory volume issued in honour of the nuptials of the Prince of Wales.

1738 *Sept.* Left Cambridge for his father's house in London without taking a degree, intending to read for the Bar at the Inner Temple in London.

1739 *Mar.* Accompanied Horace Walpole on a two-year Grand Tour through France and Italy. Visited Paris, Rheims, Dijon, Lyon, Grande Chartreuse, Geneva, Turin, Genoa, Bologna, Florence.

1740 Visited Rome, Naples and Venice. During this period Gray sent several Latin poems to West. Began writing *De Principiis Cogitandi* in Florence.

1741 *3 May* Quarrelled with Walpole at Reggio. Returned to England alone via Padua, Verona, Milan, Turin, Lyon, and Paris.
21 Aug. Visited the Grande Chartreuse again and wrote an Alcaic Ode in the Visitors' Book of the Monastery.
1 Sept. Arrived back in England.

6 Nov. Gray's father died, leaving the family in a poor financial state.

Winter Gray began his only tragedy, *Agrippina*, which he left unfinished.

1742   Intended to study law in London with West. Regular correspondence with West, exchanging Latin verses and translations with him.

Mar. Wrote the 'Hymn to Ignorance' (fragment).

May-Oct. Visited his uncle Jonathan Rogers at Stoke Poges. Wrote the 'Ode on the Spring', which he sent to Richard West on 3rd June.

1 June Richard West, Gray's closest friend, died.

Aug. Wrote the 'Ode on a Distant Prospect of Eton College', 'Sonnet on the Death of Richard West', and the 'Ode to Adversity'.

15 Oct. Returned to Peterhouse, as a Fellow-commoner, and took up permanent residence in Cambridge for the rest of his life. Gray's chief friends at Cambridge were Thomas Wharton, Fellow of Pembroke until his marriage in 1747, James Brown, afterwards Master of Pembroke, and William Mason (1724-97).

21 Oct. Death of Gray's uncle, Jonathan Rogers.

Dec. Gray's mother and her sister, Mary Antrobus, retired from Cornhill and settled with their third sister, Anne (1676-1758), the widow of Jonathan Rogers, at West End House, Stoke Poges.

1743   *Dec.* Awarded a Bachelor of Laws degree.

1745   *8 Nov.* Reconciliation with Horace Walpole.

1746   *Autumn* Gray shared some of his earlier poetry, and possibly the opening verses of the 'Elegy'—which he had recently begun— with Horace Walpole, who had moved to an apartment in the precincts of Windsor Castle.

1747   *1 Mar.* Sent the 'Ode on the Death of a Favourite Cat, Drowned in a Tub of Gold Fishes' to Walpole.

30 May 'Ode on a Distant Prospect of Eton College' published anonymously by Robert Dodsley.

Walpole leased the estate at Strawberry Hill, Twickenham, which he then began converting into a Gothic mansion.

1748   *15 Jan.* 'Ode on a Distant Prospect of Eton College', 'Ode on the Death of a Favourite Cat, Drowned in a Tub of Gold Fishes', and 'Ode on the Spring' published anonymously in R. Dodsley's *Collection of Poems*, vol. II

Jan.-Feb. Met and befriended Rev. William Mason who became a fellow of Pembroke College in 1749 and was to serve as Gray's literary executor.

Aug. Began 'The Alliance of Education and Government'

1749 William Mason elected Fellow of Pembroke.

5 Nov. Death of Gray's aunt, Mary Antrobus.

1750 *12 Jun.* Completed the 'Elegy' at Stoke Poges and sent it to Walpole who circulated it in manuscript among his friends.

Aug.-Oct. Wrote 'A Long Story' for Lady Cobham, a neighbour at Stoke Poges. Met Henrietta Jane Speed (1728-1783).

1751 *15 Feb. An Elegy Wrote in a Country Church Yard* published anonymously by Dodsley. Unauthorised versions appear in several publications.

1752 Planned to collaborate with William Mason on a *History of English Poetry.*

July Began 'The Progress of Poesy'.

1753 *11 Mar.* Death of Gray's mother, Dorothy, at Stoke Poges.

29 Mar. Designs by Mr. R. Bentley for Six Poems by Mr. T. Gray, the first authorised edition of Gray's poetry, published by Dodsley.

1754-5 Gray wrote the Pindaric Odes 'The Progress of Poesy' and 'The Bard'. Probably also began 'Ode on the Pleasure arising from Vicissitude'.

Dec. Completes 'The Progress of Poesy'.

1755 Declined offer to become Secretary to the Earl of Bristol at Lisbon.

1756 *Mar.* Moved from Peterhouse to Pembroke College.

1757 *May* Completes 'The Bard'.

8 Aug. Odes by Mr. Gray ('The Progress of Poesy' and 'The Bard') published by Walpole at his new Strawberry Hill press.

15 Dec. Offered, but refused, the post of Poet Laureate, after the death of Colley Cibber.

1758 *Jan.* Wrote '[Epitaph on Mrs. Clerke]' for John Clerke. Wrote 'Epitaph on a Child' for Thomas Wharton.

1 Sept. Gray's aunt died in Stoke Poges.

1759 *9 July* Took lodgings in Southampton Row, London, in order to study at the British Museum, which was opened to the public in January. Collected materials for his projected *History of English Poetry.*

1760 Jun-Jul. Visited Henrietta Jane Speed at the home of her friend Mrs Jennings at Shiplake, Oxfordshire.

Autumn Read and studied the works of James Macpherson and later the Rev. Evan Evans.

1761 *May* Completed 'The Fatal Sisters', 'The Descent of Odin', and other imitations of Welsh and Norse poems, intending to include them in his *History of English Poetry*.
Aug. Wrote "Epitaph on Sir W. Williams".
Oct. Wrote "Song" for Miss Speed.
12 Nov. Henrietta Jane Speed married to Baron de la Perriere.

1762 *Nov.* Gray tried to secure the post of Regius Professor of Modern History at Cambridge, but Lord Bute, Chief Minister to George III, gave it to Lawrence Brockett.

1764 *Jan.-Mar.* Gray wrote 'The Candidate', a satire on the Earl of Sandwich's application for the High Stewardship of Cambridge University.

1765 *Aug.-Oct.* Made a tour in the Scottish Highlands with Lord Strathmore. Met many literary figures in Edinburgh. Stayed at Glamis castle, where he met James Beattie (1735-1803).

1768 *Mar.* Collected edition of *Poems* published by Dodsley in London.
May Poems published by R. and A. Foulis in Glasgow.
Jul. Wrote verses 'On L[or]d H[olland']s Seat Near M[argat]e, K[en]t'.
Jul. Appointed Regius Professor of Modern History at Cambridge, and made Fellow of Pembroke College.
Oct. Poems published in a new edition by Dodsley.

1769 *Apr.* Completed the 'Ode for Music'.
Jul. 'Ode for Music' performed at the installation of the Duke of Grafton, Chancellor of the University.

1770 *Jul.* Gray made a will, leaving all his works to William Mason.

1771 *24 Jul.* Taken ill suddenly while dining at Pembroke College.
30 Jul. Gray died of suppressed gout.
6 Aug. Buried alongside his mother and aunt in the churchyard at Stoke Poges.

1775 Publication of William Mason's *The Poems of Mr Gray, to which are prefixed Memoirs of His Life and Writings*.

POEMS

BY

MR. GRAY

(1768)

O D E

ON THE

SPRING

L O! where the rosy-bosom'd Hours,
   Fair VENUS' train, appear,
Disclose the long-expecting flowers,
   And wake the purple year!
The Attic warbler pours her throat,   5
Responsive to the cuckow's note,
The untaught harmony of spring:
While whisp'ring pleasure as they fly,
Cool Zephyrs thro' the clear blue sky,
   Their gather'd fragrance fling.   10

Where'er the oak's thick branches stretch
   A broader browner shade;
Where'er the rude and moss-grown beech
   O'er-canopies the glade,
Beside some water's rushy brink   15
With me the Muse shall sit, and think
(At ease reclin'd in rustic state)
How vain the ardour of the Crowd,
How low, how little are the Proud,
   How indigent the Great!   20

Still is the toiling hand of Care;
   The panting herds repose:
Yet hark, how thro' the peopled air
   The busy murmur glows!
The insect youth are on the wing,   25
Eager to taste the honied spring,

And float amid the liquid noon:
Some lightly o'er the current skim,
Some show their gayly-gilded trim
Quick-glancing to the sun.   *30*

To Contemplation's sober eye
Such is the race of Man:
And they that creep, and they that fly,
Shall end where they began.
Alike the Busy and the Gay   *35*
But flutter thro' life's little day,
In fortune's varying colours drest:
Brush'd by the hand of rough Mischance,
Or chill'd by age, their airy dance
They leave, in dust to rest.   *40*

Methinks I hear in accents low
The sportive kind reply:
Poor moralist! and what art thou?
A solitary fly!
Thy Joys no glittering female meets,   *45*
No hive hast thou of hoarded sweets,
No painted plumage to display:
On hasty wings thy youth is flown;
Thy sun is set, thy spring is gone—
We frolick, while 'tis May.   *50*

ODE

ON THE DEATH OF A

FAVOURITE CAT

Drowned in a Tub of Gold Fishes

’TWAS on a lofty vase's side,
  Where China's gayest art had dy'd
The azure flowers that blow;
Demurest of the tabby kind,
The pensive Selima reclin'd,   5
  Gazed on the lake below.

Her conscious tail her joy declar'd;
The fair round face, the snowy beard,
  The velvet of her paws,
Her coat, that with the tortoise vies,   10
Her ears of jet, and emerald eyes,
  She saw; and purr'd applause.

Still had she gaz'd; but 'midst the tide
Two angel forms were seen to glide,
  The Genii of the stream;   15
Their scaly armour's Tyrian hue,
Thro' richest purple to the view,
  Betray'd a golden gleam.

The hapless Nymph with wonder saw:
A whisker first and then a claw,   20
  With many an ardent wish,
She stretch'd in vain to reach the prize.
What female heart can gold despise?
  What Cat's averse to fish?

Presumptuous Maid! with looks intent   *25*
Again she stretch'd, again she bent,
   Nor knew the gulf between.
(Malignant Fate sate by, and smil'd)
The slipp'ry verge her feet beguil'd,
   She tumbled headlong in.   *30*

Eight times emerging from the flood
She mew'd to every wat'ry God,
   Some speedy aid to send.
No Dolphin came, no Nereid stirr'd:
Nor cruel *Tom*, nor *Susan* heard.   *35*
   A Fav'rite has no friend!

From hence, ye Beauties, undeceiv'd,
Know, one false step is ne'er retriev'd,
   And be with caution bold.
Not all that tempts your wand'ring eyes   *40*
And heedless hearts, is lawful prize;
   Nor all, that glisters, gold.

O D E

ON A DISTANT PROSPECT OF

ETON COLLEGE

YE distant spires, ye antique towers,
   That crown the watry glade,
Where grateful Science still adores
Her HENRY's holy Shade;
And ye, that from the stately brow   *5*
Of WINDSOR's heights th'expanse below
Of grove, of lawn, of mead survey,
Whose turf, whose shade, whose flowers among
Wanders the hoary Thames along
His silver-winding way.   *10*

   Ah happy hills, ah pleasing shade,
Ah fields belov'd in vain,
Where once my careless childhood stray'd,
A stranger yet to pain!
I feel the gales, that from ye blow,   *15*
A momentary bliss bestow,
As waving fresh their gladsome wing,
My weary soul they seem to sooth,
And, redolent of joy and youth,
To breathe a second spring.   *20*

   Say, Father THAMES, for thou hast seen
Full many a sprightly race
Disporting on thy margent green
The paths of pleasure trace,
Who foremost now delight to cleave   *25*
With pliant arm thy glassy wave?
The captive linnet which enthrall?

What idle progeny succeed
To chase the rolling circle's speed,
Or urge the flying ball?   *30*

    While some on earnest business bent
Their murm'ring labours ply
'Gainst graver hours, that bring constraint
To sweeten liberty:
Some bold adventurers disdain   *35*
The limits of their little reign,
And unknown regions dare descry:
Still as they run they look behind,
They hear a voice in every wind,
And snatch a fearful joy.   *40*

    Gay hope is theirs by fancy fed,
Less pleasing when possest;
The tear forgot as soon as shed,
The sunshine of the breast:
Theirs buxom health of rosy hue,   *45*
Wild wit, invention ever-new,
And lively chear of vigour born;
The thoughtless day, the easy night,
The spirits pure, the slumbers light,
That fly th'approach of morn.   *50*

    Alas! regardless of their doom,
The little victims play!
No sense have they of ills to come,
Nor care beyond to-day:
Yet see how all around 'em wait   *55*
The Ministers of human fate,
And black Misfortune's baleful train!
Ah, shew them where in ambush stan
To seize their prey, the murth'rous band!
Ah, tell them they are men!   *60*

These shall the fury Passions tear,
The vulturs of the mind,
Disdainful Anger, pallid Fear,
And Shame that skulks behind;
Or pineing Love shall waste their youth,   *65*
Or Jealousy, with rankling tooth,
That inly gnaws the secret heart,
And Envy wan, and faded Care,
Grim-visag'd comfortless Despair
And Sorrow's piercing dart.   *70*

Ambition this shall tempt to rise,
Then whirl the wretch from high,
To bitter Scorn a sacrifice,
And grinning Infamy.
The stings of Falshood those shall try,   *75*
And hard Unkindness' alter'd eye,
That mocks the tear it forc'd to flow;
And keen Remorse with blood defil'd,
And moody Madness laughing wild
Amid severest woe.   *80*

Lo, in the vale of years beneath
A grisly troop are seen,
The painful family of Death,
More hideous than their Queen:
This racks the joints, this fires the veins,   *85*
That every labouring sinew strains,
Those in the deeper vitals rage:
Lo, Poverty, to fill the band,
That numbs the soul with icy hand,
And slow-consuming Age.   *90*

To each his suff'rings: all are men,
Condemn'd alike to groan;
The tender, for another's pain;
Th' unfeeling for his own.

Yet ah! why should they know their fate?   95
Since sorrow never comes too late,
And happiness too swiftly flies.
Thought would destroy their paradise.
No more; where ignorance is bliss,
'Tis folly to be wise.   100

HYMN

TO

ADVERSITY

—— Ζῆνα
τὸν φρονεῖν βροτοὺς ὁδώ—
σαντα, τῷ πάθει μαθάν
Θέντα κυρίως ἔχειν.

ÆSCHYLUS, in *Agamemnone*.

DAUGHTER of JOVE, relentless Power,
  Thou Tamer of the human breast,
Whose iron scourge and tort'ring hour,
The Bad affright, afflict the Best!
Bound in thy adamantine chain,   5
The Proud are taught to taste of pain,
And purple Tyrants vainly groan
With pangs unfelt before, unpitied and alone.

When first thy Sire to send on earth
Virtue, his darling Child, design'd   10
To thee he gave the heav'nly Birth,
And bade to form her infant mind.
Stern rugged Nurse! thy rigid lore
With patience many a year she bore:
What sorrow was, thou bad'st her know,   15
And from her own she learn'd to melt at others' woe.

Scar'd at thy frown terrific, fly
Self-pleasing Folly's idle brood,
Wild Laughter, Noise, and thoughtless Joy,
And leave us leisure to be good.   20
Light they disperse, and with them go

The summer Friend, the flatt'ring Foe;
By vain Prosperity received,
To her they vow their truth, and are again believed.

Wisdom in sable garb array'd   25
Immers'd in rapt'rous thought profound,
And Melancholy, silent maid,
With leaden eye, that loves the ground,
Still on thy solemn steps attend:
Warm Charity, the general Friend,   30
With Justice to herself severe,
And Pity, dropping soft the sadly-pleasing tear.

O gently on thy Suppliant's head,
Dread Goddess, lay thy chast'ning hand!
Not in thy Gorgon terrors clad,   35
Nor circled with the vengeful Band
(As by the Impious thou art seen)
With thund'ring voice, and threatening mien,
With screaming Horror's funeral cry,
Despair, and fell Disease, and ghastly Poverty.   40

Thy form benign, oh Goddess, wear,
Thy milder influence impart,
Thy philosophic Train be there,
To soften, not to wound my heart.
The gen'rous spark extinct revive,   45
Teach me to love, and to forgive,
Exact my own defects to scan,
What others are, to feel, and know myself a Man.

THE

PROGRESS of POESY

A PINDARIC ODE

φωνᾶντα συνετοῖσιν· ἐς
δὲ τὸ πᾶν ἑρμηνέων χατίζει.
PINDAR, *Olymp[ian Odes]. II. [85]*

Advertisement.
When the Author first published this and the following Ode, he was
advised, even by his Friends, to subjoin some few explanatory Notes;
but had too much respect for the understanding of his Readers
to take that liberty.

I. *1.*

AWAKE, Æolian lyre, awake,
And give to rapture all thy trembling strings.
From Helicon's harmonious springs
A thousand rills their mazy progress take:
The laughing flowers, that round them blow,   5
Drink life and fragrance as they flow.
Now the rich stream of music winds along,
Deep, majestic, smooth, and strong,
Thro' verdant vales, and Ceres' golden reign:
Now rowling down the steep amain,   10
Headlong, impetuous, see it pour:
The rocks, and nodding groves, rebellow to the roar.

I. 2.

Oh! Sovereign of the willing soul,
Parent of sweet and solemn-breathing airs,
Enchanting shell! the sullen Cares,   *15*
And frantic Passions hear thy soft controul.
On Thracia's hills the Lord of War,
Has curb'd the fury of his car,
And drop'd his thirsty lance, at thy command.
Perching on the sceptr'd hand   *20*
Of Jove, thy magic lulls the feather'd king
With ruffled plumes, and flagging wing:
Quench'd in dark clouds of slumber lie
The terror of his beak, and lightnings of his eye.

I. 3.

Thee the voice, the dance, obey,   *25*
Temper'd to thy warbled lay.
O'er Idalia's velvet-green
The rosy-crowned Loves are seen
On Cytherea's day
With antic Sports, and blue-ey'd Pleasures,   *30*
Frisking light in frolic measures;
Now pursuing, now retreating,
Now in circling troops they meet:
To brisk notes in cadence beating
Glance their many-twinkling feet.   *35*
Slow melting strains their Queen's approach declare:
Where'er she turns, the Graces homage pay.
With arms sublime, that float upon the air,
In gliding state she wins her easy way:
O'er her warm cheek, and rising bosom, move   *40*
The bloom of young Desire, and purple light of Love.

II. *1.*

    Man's feeble race what Ills await,
Labour, and Penury, the racks of Pain,
Disease, and Sorrow's weeping train,
And Death, sad refuge from the storms of Fate!   *45*
The fond complaint, my Song, disprove,
And justify the laws of Jove.
Say, has he giv'n in vain the heav'nly Muse?
Night, and all her sickly dews,
Her Spectres wan, and Birds of boding cry,   *50*
He gives to range the dreary sky:
Till down the eastern cliffs afar
Hyperion's march they spy, and glitt'ring shafts of war.

II. *2.*

    In climes beyond the solar road,
Where shaggy forms o'er ice-built mountains roam,   *55*
The Muse has broke the twilight-gloom,
To chear the shiv'ring Native's dull abode.
And oft, beneath the od'rous shade
Of Chili's boundless forests laid,
She deigns to hear the savage Youth repeat   *60*
In loose numbers wildly sweet
Their feather-cinctured Chiefs, and dusky Loves.
Her track, where'er the Goddess roves,
Glory pursue, and generous Shame,
Th' unconquerable Mind, and Freedom's holy flame.   *65*

II. *3.*

Woods, that wave o'er Delphi's steep,
Isles, that crown th' Egæan deep,
Fields, that cool Ilissus laves,
Or where Mæander's amber waves
In lingering Lab'rinths creep,   *70*

How do your tuneful Echo's languish,
Mute, but to the voice of Anguish?
Where each old poetic Mountain
Inspiration breath'd around:
Ev'ry shade and hallow'd Fountain   *75*
Murmur'd deep a solemn sound:
Till the sad Nine in Greece's evil hour
Left their Parnassus for the Latian plains.
Alike they scorn the pomp of tyrant-Power,
And coward Vice, that revels in her chains.   *80*
When Latium had her lofty spirit lost,
They sought, oh Albion! next thy sea-encircled coast.

III. *1.*

    Far from the sun and summer-gale,
In thy green lap was Nature's Darling laid,
What time, where lucid Avon stray'd,   *85*
To Him the mighty Mother did unveil
Her awful face: The dauntless Child
Stretch'd forth his little arms, and smiled.
This pencil take (she said) whose colours clear
Richly paint the vernal year: *90*
Thine too these golden keys, immortal Boy!
This can unlock the gates of Joy;
Of Horror that, and thrilling Fears,
Or ope the sacred source of sympathetic Tears.

III. *2.*

    Nor second He, that rode sublime   *95*
Upon the seraph-wings of Extasy,
The secrets of th' Abyss to spy.
He pass'd the flaming bounds of Place and Time:
The living Throne, the saphire-blaze,
Where angels tremble, while they gaze,   *100*
He saw; but, blasted with excess of light,

Closed his eyes in endless night.
Behold, where Dryden's less presumptuous car,
Wide o'er the fields of Glory bear
Two Coursers of ethereal race,   *105*
With necks in thunder cloath'd, and long-resounding pace.

III. *3.*

Hark, his hands the lyre explore!
Bright-eyed Fancy hovering o'er,
Scatters from her pictur'd urn
Thoughts, that breath, and words that burn.   *110*
But ah! 'tis heard no more——
Oh! Lyre divine, what daring Spirit
Wakes thee now? tho' he inherit
Nor the pride, nor ample pinion,
That the Theban Eagle bear,   *115*
Sailing with supreme dominion
Thro' the azure deep of air:
Yet oft before his infant eyes would run
Such forms, as glitter in the Muse's ray
With orient hues, unborrow'd of the Sun: *120*
Yet shall he mount, and keep his distant way
Beyond the limits of a vulgar fate,
Beneath the Good how far——but far above the Great.

THE

BARD

A PINDARIC ODE

Advertisement.
The following Ode is founded on a Tradition current in Wales, that
EDWARD the First, when he compleated the conquest of that country,
ordered all the Bards, that fell into his hands, to be put to death.

I. *1.*

' R UIN seize thee, ruthless King!
   'Confusion on thy banners wait,
' Tho' fann'd by Conquest's crimson wing
' They mock the air with idle state.
' Helm, nor Hauberk's twisted mail,   5
' Nor even thy virtues, Tyrant, shall avail
' To save thy secret soul from nightly fears,
' From Cambria's curse, from Cambria's tears!'
Such were the sounds, that o'er the crested pride
Of the first Edward scatter'd wild dismay,   10
As down the steep of Snowdon's shaggy side
He wound with toilsome march his long array.
Stout Gloster stood aghast in speechless trance:
To arms! cried Mortimer, and couch'd his quiv'ring lance.

I. *2.*

  On a rock, whose haughty brow   15
Frowns o'er old Conway's foaming flood,
Robed in the sable garb of woe,

With haggard eyes the Poet stood;
(Loose his beard, and hoary hair
Stream'd, like a meteor, to the troubled air)   *20*
And with a Master's hand, and Prophet's fire,
Struck the deep sorrows of his lyre.
' Hark, how each giant-oak, and desert cave,
' Sighs to the torrent's aweful voice beneath!
' O'er thee, oh King! their hundred arms they wave,   *25*
' Revenge on thee in hoarser murmurs breathe;
' Vocal no more, since Cambria's fatal day,
' To high-born Hoel's harp, or soft Llewellyn's lay.

I. 3.

  ' Cold is Cadwallo's tongue,
' That hush'd the stormy main: *30*
' Brave Urien sleeps upon his craggy bed:
' Mountains, ye mourn in vain
' Modred, whose magic song
' Made huge Plinlimmon bow his cloud-top'd head.
' On dreary Arvon's shore they lie,   *35*
' Smear'd with gore, and ghastly pale:
' Far, far aloof th' affrighted ravens sail;
' The famish'd Eagle screams, and passes by.
' Dear lost companions of my tuneful art,
' Dear, as the light, that visits these sad eyes,   *40*
' Dear, as the ruddy drops that warm my heart,
' Ye died, amidst your dying country's cries——
' No more I weep. They do not sleep.
' On yonder cliffs, a griesly band,
' I see them sit, they linger yet,   *45*
' Avengers of their native land:
' With me in dreadful harmony they join,
' And weave with bloody hands the tissue of thy line.

II. *1.*

" Weave the warp, and weave the woof,
" The winding-sheet of Edward's race.   *50*
" Give ample room, and verge enough
" The characters of hell to trace.
" Mark the year, and mark the night,
" When Severn shall re-eccho with affright
" The shrieks of death, thro' Berkley's roofs that ring,   *55*
" Shrieks of an agonizing King!
" She-Wolf of France, with unrelenting fangs,
" That tear'st the bowels of thy mangled Mate,
" From thee be born, who o'er thy country hangs
" The scourge of Heav'n. What Terrors round him wait!   *60*
" Amazement in his van, with Flight combined,
" And sorrow's faded form, and solitude behind.

II. *2.*

" Mighty Victor, mighty Lord,
" Low on his funeral couch he lies!
" No pitying heart, no eye, afford   *65*
" A tear to grace his obsequies.
" Is the sable Warriour fled?
" Thy son is gone. He rests among the Dead.
" The Swarm, that in thy noon-tide beam were born?
" Gone to salute the rising Morn.   *70*
" Fair laughs the Morn, and soft the Zephyr blows,
" While proudly riding o'er the azure realm
" In gallant trim the gilded Vessel goes;
" Youth on the prow, and Pleasure at the helm;
" Regardless of the sweeping Whirlwind's sway,   *75*
" That, hush'd in grim repose, expects his evening-prey.

II. *3.*

" Fill high the sparkling bowl,
" The rich repast prepare,
" Reft of a crown, he yet may share the feast:
" Close by the regal chair   *80*
" Fell Thirst and Famine scowl
" A baleful smile upon their baffled Guest.
" Heard ye the din of battle bray,
" Lance to lance, and horse to horse?
" Long Years of havock urge their destined course,   *85*
" And thro' the kindred squadrons mow their way.
" Ye Towers of Julius, London's lasting shame,
" With many a foul and midnight murther fed,
" Revere his Consort's faith, his Father's fame,
" And spare the meek Usurper's holy head.   *90*
" Above, below, the rose of snow,
" Twined with her blushing foe, we spread:
" The bristled Boar, in infant-gore,
" Wallows beneath the thorny shade.
" Now, Brothers, bending o'er th' accursed loom,   *95*
" Stamp we our vengeance deep, and ratify his doom.

III. *1.*

" Edward, lo! to sudden fate
" (Weave we the woof. The thread is spun)
" Half of thy heart we consecrate.
" (The web is wove. The work is done.)"   *100*
' Stay, oh stay! nor thus forlorn
' Leave me unblessed, unpitied, here to mourn:
' In yon bright track, that fires the western skies,
' They melt, they vanish from my eyes.
' But oh! what solemn scenes on Snowdon's height   *105*
' Descending slow their glitt'ring skirts unroll?
' Visions of glory! spare my aching sight,

' Ye unborn Ages, crowd not on my soul!
' No more our long-lost Arthur we bewail.
' All-hail, ye genuine Kings, Britannia's issue, hail!   *110*

III. *2.*

  ' Girt with many a Baron bold
' Sublime their starry fronts they rear;
' And gorgeous Dames, and Statesmen old
' In bearded majesty, appear.
' In the midst, a Form divine!   *115*
' Her eye proclaims her of the Briton-line;
' Her lyon-port, her awe-commanding face,
' Attemper'd sweet to virgin-grace.
' What strings symphonious tremble in the air,
' What strains of vocal transport round her play!   *120*
' Hear from the grave, great Taliessin, hear;
' They breathe a soul to animate thy clay.
' Bright Rapture calls, and soaring, as she sings,
' Waves in the eye of heav'n her many-colour'd wings.

III. *3.*

  ' The verse adorn again   *125*
' Fierce War, and faithful Love,
' And Truth severe, by fairy Fiction drest.
' In buskin'd measures move
' Pale Grief, and pleasing Pain,
' With Horror, Tyrant of the throbbing breast.   *130*
' A Voice, as of the Cherub-Choir,
' Gales from blooming Eden bear;
' And distant warblings lessen on my ear,
' That lost in long futurity expire.
' Fond impious Man, think'st thou, yon sanguine cloud,   *135*
' Rais'd by thy breath, has quench'd the Orb of day?

' To-morrow he repairs the golden flood,
' And warms the nations with redoubled ray.
' Enough for me: With joy I see
' The different doom our Fates assign.   *140*
' Be thine Despair, and scept'red Care,
' To triumph, and to die, are mine.'
He spoke, and headlong from the mountain's height
Deep in the roaring tide he plung'd to endless night.

THE

FATAL SISTERS

AN ODE

(FROM THE NORSE-TONGUE)

IN THE

ORCADES OF THORMODUS TORFÆUS
HAFNIÆ, 1697, FOLIO: AND ALSO IN
BARTHOLINUS.

VITT ER ORPIT FYRIR VALFALLI, &c.

ADVERTISEMENT.

The Author once had thoughts, in concert with a Friend, of giving *the History of English Poetry*: In the introduction to it he meant to have produced some specimens of the stile, that reigned in antient times among the neighbouring nations, or those who had subdued the greater part of this Island, and were our Progenitors. The following three imitations made a part of them. He has long since drop'd his design; especially after he had heard, that it was already in the hands of a Person well qualified to do it justice, both by his taste, and his researches into antiquity.

Preface

In the eleventh century, *Sigurd,* Earl of the Orkney-Islands went, with a fleet of ships, and a considerable body of troops, into Ireland, to the assistance of *Sictryg with the silken beard,* who was then making war on his father-in-law *Brian,* King of Dublin. The Earl and all his forces were cut to pieces, and *Sictryg* was in danger of a total defeat: but the enemy had a greater loss by the death of Brian their King, who fell in the action. On Christmas-day (the day of the battle) a Native of *Caithness* in Scotland saw, at a distance, a number of persons, on horseback, riding full speed towards a hill, and seeming to enter into it. Curiosity led him to follow them; till, looking through an opening in the rocks, he saw twelve gigantic figures resembling women: they were all employed about a loom, and, as they wove, they sung the following dreadful Song; which when they had finished, they tore the web into twelve pieces, and, each taking her portion, galloped Six to the North, and as many to the South.

Now the storm begins to lower,
(Haste, the loom of Hell prepare,)
Iron-sleet of arrowy shower
Hurtles in the darken'd air.

Glitt'ring lances are the loom,   5
Where the dusky warp we strain,
Weaving many a Soldier's doom,
Orkney's woe, and *Randver*'s bane.

See the griesly texture grow,
('Tis of human entrails made,)   10
And the weights, that play below,
Each a gasping Warriour's head.

Shafts for shuttles, dipt in gore,
Shoot the trembling cords along.
Sword, that once a Monarch bore,   15
Keep the tissue close and strong.

Mista, black terrific maid,
Sangrida, and *Hilda*, see!
Join the wayward work to aid:
'Tis the woof of victory.   20

Ere the ruddy sun be set,
Pikes must shiver, javelins sing,
Blade with clattering buckler meet,
Hauberk crash, and helmet ring.

(Weave the crimson web of war)   25
Let us go, and let us fly,
Where our Friends the conflict share,
Where they triumph, where they die.

As the paths of fate we tread,
Wading thro' th' ensanguin'd field,   30

Gondula, and *Geira*, spread
O'er the youthful King your shield.

We the reins to slaughter give,
Ours to kill, and ours to spare:
Spite of danger he shall live.   *35*
(Weave the crimson web of war.)

They, whom once the desart-beach
Pent within its bleak domain,
Soon their ample sway shall stretch
O'er the plenty of the plain.   *40*

Low the dauntless Earl is laid,
Gored with many a gaping wound:
Fate demands a nobler head;
Soon a King shall bite the ground.

Long his loss shall Eirin weep,   *45*
Ne'er again his likeness see;
Long her strains in sorrow steep,
Strains of Immortality!

Horror covers all the heath,
Clouds of carnage blot the sun.   *50*
Sisters, weave the web of death;
Sisters, cease, the work is done.

Hail the task, and hail the hands!
Songs of joy and triumph sing!
Joy to the victorious bands,   *55*
Triumph to the younger King.

Mortal, thou that hear'st the tale,
Learn the tenor of our song.
Scotland, thro' each winding vale,
Far and wide the notes prolong.   *60*

Sisters, hence with spurs of speed:
Each her thundering faulchion wield;
Each bestride her sable steed.
Hurry, hurry to the field!

THE

DESCENT of ODIN

AN ODE

(From the NORSE-TONGUE)

IN

BARTHOLINUS, *De causis contemnendae mortis*;
HAFNIÆ, 1689, Quarto.

UPREIS ODINN ALLDA GAUTR, &C.

U prose the King of Men with speed,
　And saddled strait his coal-black steed;
Down the yawning steep he rode,
That leads to HELA's drear abode.
Him the Dog of Darkness spied,　　　　　　　5
His shaggy throat he open'd wide,
While from his jaws, with carnage fill'd,
Foam and human gore distill'd;
Hoarse he bays with hideous din,
Eyes that glow, and fangs, that grin;　　　　10
And long pursues, with fruitless yell,
The Father of the powerful spell.
Onward still his way he takes
(The groaning earth beneath him shakes,)
Till full before his fearless eyes　　　　　15
The portals nine of hell arise.

Right against the eastern gate,
By the moss-grown pile he sate;
Where long of yore to sleep was laid
The dust of the prophetic Maid. 20
Facing to the northern clime,
Thrice he traced the Runic rhyme;
Thrice pronounc'd, in accents dread,
The thrilling verse that wakes the Dead:
Till from out the hollow ground 25
Slowly breath'd a sullen sound.

PROPHETESS.
What call unknown, what charms presume
To break the quiet of the tomb?
Who thus afflicts my troubled sprite,
And drags me from the realms of night? 30
Long on these mould'ring bones have beat
The winter's snow, the summer's heat,
The drenching dews, and driving rain!
Let me, let me sleep again.
Who is he, with voice unblest, 35
That calls me from the bed of rest?

ODIN.
A Traveller, to thee unknown,
Is he that calls, a Warriour's Son.
Thou the deeds of light shalt know;
Tell me what is done below, 40
For whom yon glitt'ring board is spread,
Drest for whom yon golden bed.

PROPHETESS
Mantling in the goblet see
The pure bev'rage of the bee,
O'er it hangs the shield of gold; 45
'Tis the drink of *Balder* bold.
Balder's head to death is giv'n.

Pain can reach the Sons of Heav'n!
Unwilling I my lips unclose:
Leave me, leave me to repose.   *50*

ODIN.
Once again my call obey.
Prophetess, arise, and say,
What dangers *Odin*'s Child await,
Who the Author of his fate.

PROPHETESS.
In *Hoder*'s hand the Heroe's doom: *55*
His Brother sends him to the tomb.
Now my weary lips I close:
Leave me, leave me to repose.

ODIN.
Prophetess, my spell obey,
Once again arise, and say,   *60*
Who th' Avenger of his guilt,
By whom shall *Hoder*'s blood be spilt.

PROPHETESS.
In the caverns of the west,
By *Odin*'s fierce embrace comprest,
A wond'rous boy shall *Rinda* bear,   *65*
Who ne'er shall comb his raven-hair,
Nor wash his visage in the stream,
Nor see the sun's departing beam;
Till he on *Hoder*'s corse shall smile
Flaming on the fun'ral pile.   *70*
Now my weary lips I close:
Leave me, leave me to repose.

ODIN.
Yet a while my call obey.
Prophetess, awake, and say,

What Virgins these, in speechless woe,   *75*
That bend to earth their solemn brow,
That their flaxen tresses tear,
And snowy veils, that float in air.
Tell me whence their sorrows rose:
Then I leave thee to repose.   *80*

PROPHETESS.
Ha! no Traveller art thou,
King of Men, I know thee now,
Mightiest of a mighty line——

ODIN.
No boding Maid of skill divine
Art thou, nor Prophetess of good;   *85*
But mother of the giant-brood.

PROPHETESS.
Hie thee hence, and boast at home,
That never shall Enquirer come
To break my iron-sleep again;
Till *Lok* has burst his tenfold chain.   *90*
Never, till substantial Night
Has reassum'd her antient right;
Till wrap'd in flames, in ruin hurl'd
Sinks the fabric of the world.

THE

TRIUMPHS of OWEN

A FRAGMENT

FROM

Mr Evans's Specimens of the Welch Poetry;
London, 1764, Quarto

Advertisement.

Owen succeeded his Father Griffin in the Principality of North-Wales, A.D. 1120. This battle was fought near forty Years afterwards.

O wen's praise demands my song,
   Owen swift, and Owen strong,
Fairest flower of Roderic's stem,
Gwyneth's shield and Britain's gem.
He nor heaps his brooded stores,   5
Nor on all profusely pours;
Lord of every regal art,
Liberal hand, and open heart.

  Big with hosts of mighty name,
Squadrons three against him came: 10
This the force of Eirin hiding,
Side by side, as proudly riding,
On her shadow, long and gay,
Lochlin ploughs the wat'ry way;
There the Norman sails afar;   15
Catch the winds, and join the war:

Black and huge along they sweep,
Burthens of the angry deep.

    Dauntless on his native sands
The Dragon-son of Mona stands;   *20*
In glitt'ring arms and glory drest,
High he rears his ruby crest.
There the thund'ring strokes begin,
There the press, and there the din;
Talymalfra's rocky shore   *25*
Echoing to the battle's roar.
Where his glowing eye-balls turn,
Thousand Banners round him burn.
Where he points his purple spear,
Hasty, hasty Rout is there;   *30*
Marking with indignant eye
Fear to stop, and shame to fly.
There Confusion, Terror's child,
Conflict fierce, and Ruin wild,
Agony, that pants for breath,   *35*
Despair and honourable Death.

'Elegy Written in a Country Churchyard'
from *Designs by Mr. R. Bentley, for six poems by Mr. T. Gray.*
(London: R. Dodsley, 1753)
British Library Shelfmark C.57.h.5

ELEGY

WRITTEN IN A

COUNTRY CHURCH-YARD

The Curfew tolls the knell of parting day,
The lowing herd wind slowly o'er the lea,
The plowman homeward plods his weary way,
And leaves the world to darkness, and to me.

Now fades the glimmering landscape on the sight,   *5*
And all the air a solemn stillness holds,
Save where the beetle wheels his droning flight,
And drowsy tinklings lull the distant folds;

Save that from yonder ivy-mantled tow'r,
The moping owl does to the moon complain   *10*
Of such, as wand'ring near her secret bow'r,
Molest her ancient, solitary reign.

Beneath those rugged elms, that yew-tree's shade,
Where heaves the turf in many a mould'ring heap,
Each in his narrow cell for ever laid,   *15*
The rude Forefathers of the hamlet sleep.

The breezy call of incense-breathing Morn,
The swallow twitt'ring from the straw-built shed,
The cock's shrill clarion, or the echoing horn,
No more shall rouse them from their lowly bed.   *20*

For them no more the blazing hearth shall burn,
Or busy housewife ply her evening care:

No children run to lisp their sire's return,
Or climb his knees the envied kiss to share.

Oft did the harvest to their sickle yield,   *25*
Their furrow oft the stubborn glebe has broke;
How jocund did they drive their team afield!
How bow'd the woods beneath their sturdy stroke!

Let not Ambition mock their useful toil,
Their homely joys, and destiny obscure;   *30*
Nor Grandeur hear with a disdainful smile,
The short and simple annals of the poor.

The boast of heraldry, the pomp of pow'r,
And all that beauty, all that wealth e'er gave,
Awaits alike th' inevitable hour.   *35*
The paths of glory lead but to the grave.

Nor you, ye Proud, impute to These the fault,
If Mem'ry o'er their Tomb no Trophies raise,
Where thro' the long-drawn isle and fretted vault
The pealing anthem swells the note of praise.   *40*

Can storied urn or animated bust
Back to its mansion call the fleeting breath?
Can Honour's voice provoke the silent dust,
Or Flatt'ry sooth the dull cold ear of Death?

Perhaps in this neglected spot is laid   *45*
Some heart once pregnant with celestial fire;
Hands, that the rod of empire might have sway'd,
Or wak'd to extasy the living lyre.

But Knowledge to their eyes her ample page
Rich with the spoils of time did ne'er unroll;   *50*
Chill Penury repress'd their noble rage,
And froze the genial current of the soul.

Full many a gem of purest ray serene,
The dark unfathom'd caves of ocean bear:
Full many a flower is born to blush unseen,   *55*
And waste its sweetness on the desert air.

Some village-Hampden, that with dauntless breast
The little Tyrant of his fields withstood;
Some mute inglorious Milton here may rest,
Some Cromwell guiltless of his country's blood.   *60*

Th' applause of list'ning senates to command,
The threats of pain and ruin to despise,
To scatter plenty o'er a smiling land,
And read their hist'ry in a nation's eyes,

Their lot forbad: nor circumscrib'd alone   *65*
Their growing virtues, but their crimes confin'd;
Forbad to wade through slaughter to a throne,
And shut the gates of mercy on mankind,

The struggling pangs of conscious Truth to hide,
To quench the blushes of ingenuous shame,   *70*
Or heap the shrine of Luxury and Pride
With incense kindled at the Muse's flame.

Far from the madding crowd's ignoble strife,
Their sober wishes never learn'd to stray;
Along the cool sequester'd vale of life   *75*
They kept the noiseless tenor of their way.

Yet ev'n these bones from insult to protect
Some frail memorial still erected nigh,
With uncouth rhimes and shapeless sculpture deck'd,
Implores the passing tribute of a sigh.   *80*

Their name, their years, spelt by th' unletter'd muse,
The place of fame and elegy supply:

And many a holy text around she strews,
That teach the rustic moralist to die.

For who to dumb Forgetfulness a prey,   *85*
This pleasing anxious being e'er resign'd,
Left the warm precincts of the chearful day,
Nor cast one longing ling'ring look behind?

On some fond breast the parting soul relies,
Some pious drops the closing eye requires;   *90*
Ev'n from the tomb the voice of Nature cries,
Ev'n in our Ashes live their wonted Fires.

For thee, who mindful of th' unhonour'd Dead,
Dost in these lines their artless tale relate;
If chance, by lonely Contemplation led,   *95*
Some kindred Spirit shall enquire thy fate,

Haply some hoary-headed Swain may say,
' Oft have we seen him, at the peep of dawn
' Brushing with hasty steps the dews away
' To meet the sun upon the upland lawn.   *100*

' There at the foot of yonder nodding beech
' That wreathes its old fantastic roots so high,
' His listless length at noontide would he stretch,
' And pore upon the brook that babbles by.

' Hard by yon wood, now smiling as in scorn,   *105*
' Mutt'ring his wayward fancies he would rove,
' Now drooping, woeful wan, like one forlorn,
' Or craz'd with care, or cross'd in hopeless love.

' One morn I miss'd him on the custom'd hill,
' Along the heath and near his fav'rite tree;   *110*
' Another came; nor yet beside the rill,
' Nor up the lawn, nor at the wood was he;

' The next with dirges due, in sad array
' Slow thro' the church-way path we saw him born.
' Approach, and read (for thou can'st read) the lay,   *115*
' Grav'd on his stone, beneath yon aged thorn.'

The EPITAPH

Here rests his head upon the lap of earth
A Youth to Fortune and to Fame unknown.
Fair Science frown'd not on his humble birth,
And Melancholy mark'd him for her own.   *120*

Large was his bounty, and his soul sincere,
Heav'n did a recompence as largely send:
He gave to Mis'ry all he had, a tear,
He gain'd from Heav'n ('twas all he wish'd) a friend.

No farther seek his merits to disclose,   *125*
Or draw his frailties from their dread abode,
(There they alike in trembling hope repose,)
The bosom of his Father and his God.

Six Poems

BY

M R T G RAY

(1753)

A Long STORY.

In Britain's Isle, no matter where,
  An ancient pile of building stands;
The Huntingdons and Hattons there
Employ'd the power of Fairy hands

To raise the cieling's fretted height,   *5*
Each pannel in achievements cloathing,
Rich windows that exclude the light,
And passages, that lead to nothing.

Full oft within the spacious walls,
When he had fifty winters o'er him,   *10*
My grave Lord-Keeper led the Brawls:
The Seal, and Maces, danc'd before him.

His bushy beard, and shoe-strings green,
His high-crown'd hat, and sattin-doublet,
Mov'd the stout heart of England's Queen,   *15*
Tho' Pope and Spaniard could not trouble it.

What, in the very first beginning!
Shame of the versifying tribe!
Your Hist'ry whither are you spinning?
Can you do nothing but describe?   *20*

A House there is, (and that's enough)
From whence one fatal morning issues
A brace of Warriors, not in buff,
But rustling in their silks and tissues.

The first came cap-a-pee from France   *25*
Her conqu'ring destiny fulfilling,
Whom meaner beauties eye askance,
And vainly ape her art of killing.

The other Amazon kind Heaven
Had arm'd with spirit, wit, and satire: *30*
But COBHAM had the polish given,
And tip'd her arrows with good-nature.

To celebrate her eyes, her air———
Coarse panegyricks would but teaze her.
Melissa is her Nom de Guerre.   *35*
Alas, who would not wish to please her!

With bonnet blue and capucine,
And aprons long they hid their armour,
And veil'd their weapons bright and keen
In pity to the country-farmer.   *40*

Fame in the shape of Mr. P———t
(By this time all the Parish know it)
Had told, that thereabouts there lurk'd
A wicked Imp they call a Poet,

Who prowl'd the country far and near,   *45*
Bewitch'd the children of the peasants,
Dried up the cows, and lam'd the deer,
And suck'd the eggs, and kill'd the pheasants.

My Lady heard their joint petition,
Swore by her coronet and ermine,   *50*
She'd issue out her high commission
To rid the manour of such vermin.

The Heroines undertook the task,
Thro' lanes unknown, o'er stiles they ventur'd,
Rap'd at the door, nor stay'd to ask,   *55*
But bounce into the parlour enter'd.

The trembling family they daunt,
They flirt, they sing, they laugh, they tattle,

Rummage his Mother, pinch his Aunt,
And up stairs in a whirlwind rattle.   *60*

Each hole and cupboard they explore,
Each creek and cranny of his chamber,
Run hurry-skurry round the floor,
And o'er the bed and tester clamber,

Into the Drawers and China pry,   *65*
Papers and books, a huge Imbroglio!
Under a tea-cup he might lie,
Or creased, like dogs-ears, in a folio.

On the first marching of the troops
The Muses, hopeless of his pardon,   *70*
Convey'd him underneath their hoops
To a small closet in the garden.

So Rumor says. (Who will, believe.)
But that they left the door a-jarr,
Where, safe and laughing in his sleeve,   *75*
He heard the distant din of war.

Short was his joy. He little knew,
The power of Magick was no fable.
Out of the window, whisk, they flew,
But left a spell upon the table.   *80*

The words too eager to unriddle,
The Poet felt a strange disorder:
Transparent birdlime form'd the middle,
And chains invisible the border.

So cunning was the Apparatus,   *85*
The powerful pothooks did so move him,
That, will he, nill he, to the Great-house
He went, as if the Devil drove him.

Yet on his way (no sign of grace,
For folks in fear are apt to pray)   *90*
To Phœbus he prefer'd his case,
And beg'd his aid that dreadful day.

The Godhead would have back'd his quarrel,
But with a blush on recollection
Own'd, that his quiver and his laurel   *95*
'Gainst four such eyes were no protection.

The Court was sate, the Culprit there,
Forth from their gloomy mansions creeping
The Lady *Janes* and *Joans* repair,
And from the gallery stand peeping: *100*

Such as in silence of the night
Come (sweep) along some winding entry
(*Styack* has often seen the sight)
Or at the chappel-door stand sentry;

In peaked hoods and mantles tarnish'd,   *105*
Sour visages, enough to scare ye,
High Dames of honour once, that garnish'd
The drawing-room of fierce Queen Mary!

The Peeress comes. The Audience stare,
And doff their hats with due submission: *110*
She curtsies, as she takes her chair,
To all the People of condition.

The Bard with many an artful fib,
Had in imagination fenc'd him,
Disproved the arguments of *Squib*,   *115*
And all that *Groom* could urge against him.

But soon his rhetorick forsook him,
When he the solemn hall had seen;

A sudden fit of ague shook him,
He stood as mute as poor *Macleane*.   *120*

Yet something he was heard to mutter,
' How in the park beneath an old-tree
' (Without design to hurt the butter,
' Or any malice to the poultry,)

' He once or twice had pen'd a sonnet;   *125*
' Yet hoped, that he might save his bacon:
' Numbers would give their oaths upon it,
' He ne'er was for a conj'rer taken.'

The ghostly Prudes with hagged face
Already had condemn'd the sinner.   *130*
My Lady rose, and with a grace——
She smiled, and bid him come to dinner.

' Jesu-Maria! Madam Bridget,
' Why, what can the Viscountess mean?
(Cried the square hoods in woful fidget)   *135*
' The times are altered quite and clean!

' Decorum's turn'd to mere civility;
' Her air and all her manners shew it.
' Commend me to her affability!
' Speak to a Commoner and Poet!"   *140*

        [Here 500 Stanzas are lost.]

And so God save our noble King,
And guard us from long-winded Lubbers,
That to eternity would sing,
And keep my Lady from her Rubbers.

ODE

FOR

MUSIC

Air

"Hence, avaunt, ('tis holy ground)
"Comus and his midnight-crew,
"And Ignorance with looks profound,
"And dreaming Sloth of pallid hue,
"Mad Sedition's cry profane,   5
"Servitude that hugs her chain,
"Nor in these consecrated bowers
"Let painted Flatt'ry hide her serpent-train in flowers.

Chorus

"Nor Envy base nor creeping Gain
"Dare the Muse's walk to stain,   10
"While bright-eyed Science watches round:
"Hence, away, 'tis holy ground!"

Recitative

From yonder realms of empyrean day
Bursts on my ear th' indignant lay:
There sit the sainted Sage, the Bard divine,   15
The Few, whom Genius gave to shine
Through every unborn age, and undiscovered clime.
Rapt in celestial transport they,   *(accomp.)*
Yet hither oft a glance from high
They send of tender sympathy   20
To bless the place, where on their opening soul
First the genuine ardor stole.
'Twas *Milton* struck the deep-toned shell,

And, as the choral warblings round him swell,
Meek *Newton's* self bends from his state sublime,   25
And nods his hoary head and listens to the rhyme.

                    AIR
"Ye brown o'er-arching groves,
"That Contemplation loves,
"Where willowy *Camus* lingers with delight!
"Oft at the blush of dawn   30
"I trod your level lawn,
"Oft woo'd the gleam of *Cynthia* silver-bright
"In cloisters dim, far from the haunts of Folly,
"With Freedom by my Side, and soft-ey'd Melancholy."

                    RECITATIVE
But hark! the portals sound, and pacing forth   35
With solemn steps and slow,
High Potentates and Dames of royal birth
And mitred Fathers in long order go:
Great *Edward* with the lillies on his brow
From haughty *Gallia* torn,   40
And sad *Chatillon*, on her bridal morn
That wept her bleeding Love, and princely *Clare*,
And *Anjou's* Heroïne, and the paler Rose,
The rival of her crown and of her woes,
And either *Henry* there,   45
The murther'd Saint, and the majestic Lord,
That broke the bonds of *Rome*,
(Their tears, their little triumphs o'er,   *(accomp.)*
Their human passions now no more,
Save Charity, that glows beyond the tomb).   50
All that on *Granta's* fruitful plain
Rich streams of regal bounty pour'd,
And bad these awful fanes and turrets rise,
To hail their *Fitzroy's* festal morning come;
And thus they speak in soft accord   55
The liquid language of the skies.

QUARTETTO
"What is Grandeur, what is Power?
"Heavier toil, superior pain.
"What the bright reward we gain?
"The grateful mem'ry of the Good.   *60*
"Sweet is the breath of vernal shower,
"The bee's collected treasures sweet,
"Sweet music's melting fall, but sweeter yet
"The still small voice of Gratitude."

RECITATIVE
Foremost and leaning from her golden cloud   *65*
The venerable *Marg'ret* see!
"Welcome, my noble Son, (she cries aloud)
"To this, thy kindred train, and me:
"Pleased in thy lineaments we trace
"A *Tudor's* fire, a *Beaufort's* grace.   *70*

AIR
"Thy liberal heart, thy judging eye,
"The flower unheeded shall descry,
"And bid it round heaven's altars shed
"The fragrance of it's blushing head:
"Shall raise from earth the latent gem   *75*
"To glitter on the diadem.

RECITATIVE
"Lo, *Granta* waits to lead her blooming band,
"Not obvious, not obtrusive, She
"No vulgar praise, no venal incense flings;
"Nor dares with courtly tongue refin'd   *80*
"Profane thy inborn royalty of mind:
"She reveres herself and thee.
"With modest pride to grace thy youthful brow
"The laureate wreath, that *Cecil* wore, she brings,
"And to thy just, thy gentle hand
85

"Submits the Fasces of her sway,
"While Spirits blest above and Men below
"Join with glad voice the loud symphonious lay.

    GRAND CHORUS
"Thro' the wild waves as they roar
"With watchful eye and dauntless mien   *90*
"Thy steady course of honor keep,
"Nor fear the rocks, nor seek the shore:
"The Star of *Brunswick* smiles serene,
"And gilds the horrors of the deep."

ON L[OR]D H[OLLAND']S SEAT
NEAR M[ARGAT]E, K[EN]T

Old and abandon'd by each venal friend,
 Here H[ollan]d took the pious resolution,
To smuggle some few years, and strive to mend
 A broken character and constitution.
On this congenial spot he fix'd his choice;   *5*
 Earl Godwin trembled for his neighbouring sand,
Here Seagulls scream, and cormorants rejoice,
 And mariners, tho' shipwreckt dread to land.
Here reign the blustring North and blighting East,
 No tree is heard to whisper, bird to sing,   *10*
Yet nature could not furnish out the feast,
 Art he invokes new terrors still to bring:
Now mouldring fanes and battlements arise,
 Arches and turrets nodding to their fall,
Unpeopled palaces delude his eyes,   *15*
 And mimick desolation covers all.
Ah! said the sighing peer, "had Bute been true,
 Nor Shelburn's, Rigby's, Calcraft's friendship vain,
Far other scenes than these had bless'd our view,
 And realis'd the beauties that we feign.   *20*
Purg'd by the sword, and beautifyed by fire,
 Then had we seen proud London's hated walls,
Owls might have hooted in St Peter's Quire,
 And foxes stunk and litter'd in St Pauls.

Appendix

STANZA'S WROTE IN A COUNTRY CHURCH-YARD

(The Eton Manuscript)

The Curfeu tolls the Knell of parting Day,
The lowing Herd winds slowly o'er the Lea,
The Plowman homeward plods his weary Way,
And leaves the World to Darkness & to me.

Now fades the glimm'ring Landscape on the Sight,   *5*
And all the Air a solemn Stillness holds;
Save, where the Beetle wheels his droning Flight,
Or drowsy Tinklings lull the distant Folds.

Save, that from yonder ivy-mantled Tower
The mopeing Owl does to the Moon complain   *10*
Of such as wandring[1] near her secret Bower,
Molest her ancient[2] solitary Reign.

Beneath those rugged Elms, that Yewtree's Shade,
Where heaves the Turf in many a mould'ring Heap,
Each in his narrow Cell for ever laid,   *15*
The rude Forefathers of the Hamlet[3] sleep.

For ever sleep, the breezy Call of Morn,
Or Swallow twitt'ring from the strawbuilt Shed,
Or Chaunticleer so shrill or ecchoing Horn,
No more shall rouse them from their lowly Bed.   *20*

---

[1] "stray" is inserted above the word "wandring".
[2] "& pry into" is written above "Molest her ancient".
[3] "Village" is scored through and "Hamlet" written in above.

For them no more the blazeing Hearth shall burn,
Or busy Huswife ply her Evening Care;
No Children run to lisp their Sire's Return,
Or climb his Knees the coming[4] Kiss to share.

Oft did the Harvest to their Sickle yield;   *25*
Their Furrow oft the stubborn Glebe has broke;
How jocund did they they drive their Team a-field!
How bow'd the Woods beneath their sturdy Stroke!

    Let not Ambition mock their useful[5] Toil,
Their rustic Joys & Destiny obscure: *30*
Nor Grandeur hear with a disdainful Smile,
The short & simple Annals of the Poor.

The Boast of Heraldry the Pomp of Power,
And all, that Beauty, all that Wealth, e'er gave
Awaits alike th' inevitable Hour.   *35*
The Paths of Glory lead but to the Grave.

    Forgive, ye Proud, th' involuntary Fault,
If Memory to these no Trophies raise,
Where thro' the long-drawn Ile, & fretted Vault
The pealing Anthem swells the Note of Praise.   *40*

    Can storied Urn, or animated Bust
Back to its Mansion call the fleeting Breath?
Can Honour's Voice awake[6] the silent dust,
Or Flattery sooth the dull cold Ear of Death!

1. Perhaps in this neglected Spot is laid   *45*
Some Heart, once pregnant with celestial Fire,
Hands, that the Reins of Empire might have sway'd,
Or waked to Ecstasy the living Lyre:

---

[4] "envied" is written above and "doubtful?" written in the margin.
[5] "homely" is written in the margin as a replacement for "useful".
[6] "provoke" is written in the margin as a replacement for "awake".

4. Some Village Cato   [7] with dauntless Breast
The little Tyrant of his Fields withstood;   *50*
Some mute inglorious Tully here may rest;
Some Caesar, guiltless of his Country's Blood.

2. But Knowledge to their eyes her ample Page,
Rich with the Spoils of Time, did ne'er unroll:
Chill Penury had damp'd[8] their noble Rage,   *55*
And froze the genial Current of the Soul.

3. Full many a Gem of purest Ray serene
The dark unfathom'd Caves of Ocean bear.
Full many a Flower is born to blush unseen
And waste its Sweetness on the desert Air.   *60*

Th' Applause of listening Senates to command,
The Threats of Pain & Ruin to despise,
To scatter Plenty o'er a smiling Land,
And read their Hist'ry in a Nation's Eyes

Their Fate[9] forbad: nor circumscribed alone   *65*
Their struggling[10] Virtues, but their Crimes confined;
Forbad to wade thro' Slaughter to a Throne,
And shut the Gates of Mercy on Mankind

The struggleing Pangs of conscious Truth to hide,
To quench the Blushes of ingenuous Shame,   *70*
And at[11] the Shrine of Luxury and Pride
With[12] Incense hallowd in[13] the Muse's Flame.

---

[7] The space here represents a word that has been lost due to fraying of the manuscript. Commentators tend to assume that the missing word is "who".

[8] Above this word in the MS are written the words "depress'd repress'd".

[9] The MS has "Lot" inserted above "Fate".

[10] The MS has "growing" written above "struggling".

[11] Above "at" is written "crown".

[12] "Burn" is scored through and "With" written above.

[13] "Kindled at" is inserted below the line, and "by" instead of "in" above.

The thoughtless World to Majesty may bow
Exalt the brave, & idolize Success
But more to Innocence their Safety owe   75
Than Power & Genius e'er conspired to bless

And thou, who mindful of the unhonour'd Dead
Dost in these Notes their[14] artless Tale relate
By Night & lonely Contemplation led
To linger in the gloomy Walks of Fate   80

Hark how the sacred Calm, that broods around
Bids ev'ry fierce tumultuous Passion cease
In still small Accents, whisp'ring from the Ground
A grateful Earnest of eternal Peace

No more with Reason & thyself at Strife;   85
Give anxious Cares & endless Wishes room
But thro' the cool sequester'd Vale of Life
Pursue the silent Tenour of thy Doom.

Far from the madding Crowd's ignoble Strife,
Their sober Wishes never knew to stray: 90
Along the cool sequester'd Vale of Life
They kept the silent[15] Tenour of their Way.

Yet even these Bones from Insult to protect
Some frail Memorial still erected nigh
With[16] uncouth Rhime, & shapeless Sculpture deckt,   95
Implores the passing Tribute of a Sigh.

Their Name, their Years, spelt by th' unlettered Muse
The Place of Fame, & Epitaph supply

---

[14] Originally "thy", but the letter Y is scored through and "eir" inserted above.
[15] "Noiseless" is written above "silent".
[16] "With" has replaced another word in the MS, possibly "In", which has been inked out.

And many a holy Text around she strews,
That teach the rustic Moralist to die.   *100*

For who to dumb Forgetfulness, a Prey,
This pleasing anxious Being e'er resign'd;
Left the warm Precincts of the chearful Day,
Nor cast one longing lingring Look behind?

On some fond Breast the parting Soul relies,   *105*
Some pious Drops the closing Eye requires:
Even from the Tomb the Voice of Nature cries,
And buried Ashes glow with Social Fires.

For Thee, who mindful of th' unhonour'd Dead
Dost in these Notes their artless Tale relate   *110*
By Night & lonely Contemplation led
To linger in the gloomy Walks of Fate

If chance that e'er some pensive Spirit more,
By sympathetic Musings here delay'd,
With vain, tho' kind, Enquiry shall explore   *115*
Thy once-loved Haunt, this long-deserted Shade.

Haply some hoaryheaded Swain shall say,
Oft have we seen him at the Peep of Dawn
With hasty Footsteps brush the Dews away
On the high Brow of yonder yonder hanging Lawn   *120*

Him have we seen the Green-wood Side along
While o'er the Heath we hied, our Labours done,
Oft as the Woodlark piped her farewell Song
With whistful Eyes pursue the setting Sun.

Oft at the Foot of yonder hoary[1] Beech   *125*
That wreathes its old fantastic Roots so high

---

[1] "spreading" is written above "hoary"; "nodding" is written in the margin.

His listless Length at Noontide would he stretch,
And pore upon the Brook that babbles by.

With Gestures quaint now smileing as in Scorn,
Mutt'ring his fond Conceits[2] he would he[3] rove,   *130*
Now drooping, woeful wan,[4] as one forlorn,
Or crazed with care, or cross'd in hopeless Love.

One Morn we miss'd him on th' customd[5] Hill,
By[6] the Heath[7] and at[8] his fav'rite Tree;
Another came, nor yet beside the Rill,   *135*
Nor up the Lawn, nor at[9] the Wood was he.

[10]The next with Dirges meet in sad Array
Slow thro[11] the Church-way Path we saw him born.
Approach & read, for thou can'st read the Lay,
Wrote[12] on the Stone beneath that[13] ancient Thorn: *140*

There scatter'd oft the earliest of ye year[14]
By Hands unseen, are frequent[15] Vi'lets found;
The Robin[16] loves to build & warble there
And little Footsteps lightly print the ground.

---

[2] "wayward fancies" is written above "Conceits".
[3] "wont to" has been scored through; "loved" written above and also scored through; "would he" is then written above that.
[4] The line originally began "Now woeful wan, he droop'd". "Drooping" is written in above, and "he droop'd" scored through.
[5] Originally "accustomed"; "ac-" is scored through.
[6] "Along" is written above.
[7] "side" is written after "Heath" but scored through.
[8] "near" is written above "at".
[9] "By" is written above.
[10] Before this stanza is written "There scatter'd oft, the earliest", scored through.
[11] "By" is written above.
[12] The words "garved carved" are written above.
[13] "Yon" is written above.
[14] "Spring" has been struck out and "year" inserted above.
[15] "Showers of" is written above.
[16] "Redbreast" is written above.

Here[17] rests his Head upon the Lap of Earth   *145*
A Youth to Fortune & to Fame unknown
Fair Science frown'd not on his humble birth
And Melancholy mark'd him for her own

Large was his Bounty & his Heart sincere;
Heaven did a Recompence as largely send.   *150*
He gave to Mis'ry all he had, a Tear.
He gained from Heav'n; twas all he wish'd, a Friend

No further seek his Merits to disclose,
Nor seek[18] to draw them from their dread Abode,
(His frailties there in trembling Hope repose)   *155*
The Bosom of his Father & his God.

---

[17] The Epitaph is written along the outer margin, at right angles to the rest of the poem.

[18] "Think" is written above "seek".

Poems Published Posthumously

AGRIPPINA, a TRAGEDY

Dramatis Personæ.

AGRIPPINA, the Empress mother.
NERO, the Emperor.
POPPÆA, believed to be in love with OTHO.
OTHO, a young man of quality, in love with POPPÆA.
SENECA, the Emperor's preceptor.
ANICETUS, Captain of the Guards.
DEMETRIUS, the Cynic, friend to Seneca.
ACERONIA, Confidant to AGRIPPINA.

SCENE, the Emperor's villa at Baiæ

THE ARGUMENT

The drama opens with the indignation of Agrippina, at receiving her son's orders from Anicetus to remove from Baiæ, and to have her guard taken from her. At this time Otho having conveyed Poppæa from the house of her husband Rufus Crispinus, brings her to Baiæ, where he means to conceal her among the croud; or, if his fraud is discovered, to have recourse to the Emperor's authority; but, knowing the lawless temper of Nero, he determines not to have recourse to that expedient, but on the utmost necessity. In the meantime he commits her to the care of Anicetus, whom he takes to be his friend, and in whose age he thinks he may safely confide. Nero is not yet come to Baiæ: but Seneca, whom he sends before him, informs Agrippina of the accusation concerning Rubellius Plancus, and desires her to clear herself, which she does briefly; but demands to see her son, who, on his arrival, acquits her of all suspicion, and restores her to her honours. In the meanwhile Anicetus, to whose care Poppaea had been entrusted by Otho, contrives the following plot to ruin Agrippina: He betrays his trust to Otho, and brings Nero, as it were by chance, to the sight of the beautiful Poppæa; the Emperor is immediately struck with her charms, and she, by a feigned resistance, increases his passion; tho', in reality, she is from the first dazzled with the prospect of empire, and forgets Otho: She therefore joins with Anicetus in his design of ruining Agrippina, soon perceiving that it will be for her interest.

Otho hearing that the Emperor had seen Poppæa, is much enraged; but not knowing that this interview was obtained thro' the treachery of Anicetus, is readily persuaded by him to see Agrippina in secret, and acquaint her with his fears that her son Nero would marry Poppæa. Agrippina, to support her own power, and to wean the Emperor from the love of Poppæa, gives Otho encouragement, and promises to support him. Anicetus secretly introduces Nero to hear their discourse; who resolves immediately on his mother's death, and, by Anicetus's means, to destroy her by drowning. A solemn feast, in honour of their reconciliation, is to be made; after which she being to go by sea to Bauli, the ship is so contrived as to sink or crush her; she escapes by accident, and returns to Baiæ. In this interval Otho has an interview with Poppæa; and being duped a second time by Anicetus and her, determines to fly with her into Greece, by means of a vessel which is to be furnished by Anicetus; but he, pretending to remove Poppæa on board in the night, conveys her to Nero's apartment: She there encourages and determines Nero to banish Otho, and finish the horrid deed he had attempted on his mother. Anicetus undertakes to execute his resolves; and, under pretence of a plot upon the Emperor's life, is sent with a guard to murder Agrippina, who is still at Baiæ in imminent fear, and irresolute how to conduct herself. The account of her death, and the Emperor's horrour and fruitless remorse, finishes the drama.

I refer the reader to the 13th and 14th books of the annals of Tacitus for the facts on which this story is founded: By turning to that author, he will easily see how far the poet thought it necessary to deviate from the truth of history. I shall only further observe, that as such a fable could not possibly admit of any good character, it is terror only and not pity that could be excited by this tragedy, had it been completed. Yet it was surely capable of exciting this passion in a supreme degree; if, what the critics tell us be true, that crimes, which illustrious persons commit, affect us from the very circumstance of their rank, because we unite with that our fears for the public weal.

Act I. Scene I.

Agrippina, Aceronia

Agrippina

'Tis well, begone! your errand is performed:

> *[Speaks as to Anicetus entering.*

The message needs no comment. Tell your master,
His mother shall obey him. Say you saw her
Yielding due reverence to his high command:
Alone, unguarded and without a Lictor   5
As fits the daughter of Germanicus.
Say, she retired to Antium; there to tend
Her houshold cares, a woman's best employment.
What if you add, how she turned pale, and trembled;
You think, you spied a tear stand in her eye,   10
And would have drop'd, but that her pride restraine'd it?
(Go! you can paint it well) 'twill profit you,
And please the stripling. Yet 'twould dash his joy
To hear the spirit of Britannicus
Yet walks on earth; at least there are who know   15
Without a spell to raise, and bid it fire
A thousand haughty hearts, unus'd to shake
When a boy frowns, nor to be lur'd with smiles
To taste of hollow kindness, or partake
His hospitable board: They are aware   20
Of th' unpledg'd bowl, they love not Aconite.

Aceronia

He's gone; and much I hope these walls alone,
And the mute air are privy to your passion.
Forgive your servant's fears, who sees the danger
Which fierce resentment cannot fail to raise   25
In haughty youth and irritated power.

AGRIPPINA

And dost thou talk to me, to me, of danger,
Of haughty youth, and irritated power,
To her that gave it being, her that arm'd
This painted Jove, and taught his novice hand   *30*
To aim the forked bolt; while he stood trembling,
Scar'd at the sound, and dazzled with its brightness?
    'Tis like, thou hast forgot, when yet a stranger
To adoration, to the grateful steam
Of flattery's incense, and obsequious vows   *35*
From voluntary realms, a puny boy,
Decked with no other lustre, than the blood
Of Agrippina's race, he liv'd unknown
To fame, or fortune; haply eyed at distance
Some edileship, ambitious of the power   *40*
To judge of weights, and measures; scarcely dar'd
On expectation's strongest wing to soar
High as the consulate, that empty shade
Of long-forgotten liberty: when I
Oped his young eye to bear the blaze of greatness;   *45*
Showed him, where empire tower'd, and bade him strike
The noble quarry. Gods! then was the time
To shrink from danger; fear might then have worn
The mask of prudence: but a heart like mine,
A heart that glows with the pure Julian fire,   *50*
If bright Ambition from her craggy seat
Display the radiant prize, will mount undaunted,
Gain the rough heights, and grasp the dangerous honour.

ACERONIA

Thro' various life I have pursued your steps,
Have seen your soul, and wonder'd at its daring: *55*
Hence rise my fears. Nor am I yet to learn
How vast the debt of gratitude, which Nero
To such a mother owes; the world, you gave him
Suffices not to pay the obligation.
    I well remember too (for I was present)   *60*

When in a secret and dead hour of night,
Due sacrifice perform'd with barb'rous rites
Of mutter'd charms and solemn invocation,
You bade the Magi call the dreadful powers'
That read futurity, to know the fate   *65*
Impending o'er your son: Their answer was,
If the son reign, the mother perishes.
Perish (you cry'd) the mother! reign the son!
He reigns, the rest is heav'n's; who oft has bad,
Ev'n when its will seem'd wrote in lines of blood,   *70*
Th' unthought event disclose a whiter meaning.
Think too how oft in weak and sickly minds
The sweets of kindness lavishly indulg'd
Rankle to gall; and benefits too great
To be repaid, sit heavy on the soul,   *75*
As unrequited wrongs. The willing homage
Of prostrate Rome, the senate's joint applause,
The riches of the earth, the train of pleasures
That wait on youth, and arbitrary sway;
These were your gift, and with them you bestow'd   *80*
The very power he has to be ungrateful.

        AGRIPPINA
Thus ever grave and undisturb'd reflection
Pours its cool dictates in the madding ear
Of rage, and thinks to quench the fire it feels not.
Say'st thou I must be cautious, must be silent,   *85*
And tremble at the phantom I have rais'd?
Carry to him thy timid counsels. He
Perchance may heed 'em: Tell him too, that one,
Who had such liberal power to give, may still
With equal power resume that gift, and raise   *90*
A tempest, that shall shake her own creation
To its original atoms—tell me! say,
This mighty Emperor, this dreaded Hero,
Has he beheld the glittering front of war?
Knows his soft ear the Trumpet's thrilling voice,   *95*

83

And outcry of the battle? Have his limbs
Sweat under iron harness? Is he not
The silken son of dalliance, nurs'd in Ease
And Pleasure's flowery lap? Rubellius lives,
And Sylla has his friends, tho' school'd by fear   *100*
To bow the supple knee, and court the times
With shows of fair obeisance; and a call,
Like mine, might serve belike to wake pretensions
Drowsier than theirs, who boast the genuine blood
Of our imperial house. [Cannot my nod]   *105*
Rouse [up] eight hardy legions, wont to stem
With stubborn nerves the tide, and face the rigour
Of bleak Germania's snows. Four, not less brave,
That in Armenia quell the Parthian force
Under the warlike Corbulo, by [me]   *110*
Mark'd for their leader: These, by ties confirm'd,
Of old respect and gratitude, are [mine].
Surely the Masians too, and those of Egypt,
Have not forgot [my] sire: The eye of Rome
And the Praetorian camp have long rever'd,   *115*
With custom'd awe, the daughter, sister, wife,
And mother of their Caesars.
                  Ha! by Juno,
It bears a noble semblance. On this base
My great revenge shall rise; or say we sound
The trump of liberty; there will not want,   *120*
Even in the servile senate, ears to own
Her spirit-stirring voice; Soranus there,
And Cassius; Vetus too, and Thrasea,
Minds of the antique cast, rough, stubborn souls,
That struggle with the yoke. How shall the spark   *125*
Unquenchable, that glows within their breasts,
Blaze into freedom, when the idle herd
(Slaves from the womb, created but to stare,
And bellow in the Circus) yet will start,
And shake 'em at the name of liberty,   *130*
Stung by a senseless word, a vain tradition,

As there were magic in it? Wrinkled beldams
Teach it their grandchildren, as somewhat rare
That anciently appear'd, but when, extends
Beyond their chronicle—oh! 'tis a cause   *135*
To arm the hand of childhood, and rebrace
The slacken'd sinews of time-wearied age.
    Yes, we may meet, ungrateful boy, we may!
Again the buried genius of old Rome
Shall from the dust uprear his reverend head,   *140*
Rous'd by the shout of millions: There before
His high tribunal thou and I appear.
Let majesty sit on thy awful brow,
And lighten from thy eye: Around thee call
The gilded swarm that wantons in the sunshine   *145*
Of thy full favour; Seneca be there
In gorgeous phrase of labour'd eloquence
To dress thy plea, and Burrhus strengthen it
With his plain soldier's oath and honest seeming.
Against thee, liberty and Agrippina: *150*
The world, the prize; and fair befall the victors.
    But soft! why do I waste the fruitless hours
In threats unexecuted? Haste thee, fly
These hated walls that seem to mock my shame,
And cast me forth in duty to their lord.   *155*
    My thought aches at him; not the basilisk
More deadly to the sight, than is to me
The cool injurious eye of frozen kindness.
I will not meet its poison. Let him feel
Before he sees me. Yes, I will be gone,   *160*
But not to Antium—all shall be confess'd,
Whate'er the frivolous tongue of giddy fame
Has spread among the crowd; things, that but whisper'd
Have arch'd the hearer's brow, and riveted
His eyes in fearful extasy: No matter   *165*
What; so't be strange, and dreadful.—Sorceries,
Assassinations, poisonings—the deeper
My guilt, the blacker his ingratitude.

And you, ye manes of ambition's victims,
Enshrined Claudius, with the pitied ghosts   *170*
Of the Syllani, doom'd to early death
(Ye unavailing horrours, fruitless crimes!),
If from the realms of night my voice ye hear,
In lieu of penitence and vain remorse,
Accept my vengeance. Tho' by me ye bled,   *175*
He was the cause. My love, my fears for him,
Dried the soft springs of pity in my heart,
And froze them up with deadly cruelty.
Yet if your injur'd shades demand my fate,
If murder cries for murder, blood for blood,   *180*
Let me not fall alone; but crush his pride,
And sink the traitor in his mother's ruin.   *Exeunt.*

Scene II.

OTHO, POPPAEA

OTHO
Thus far we're safe. Thanks to the rosy queen
Of amorous thefts: And had her wanton son
Lent us his wings, we could not have beguil'd   *185*
With more elusive speed the dazzled sight
Of wakeful jealousy. Be gay securely;
Dispel, my fair, with smiles, the tim'rous cloud
That hangs on thy clear brow. So Helen look'd,
So her white neck reclin'd, so was she borne   *190*
By the young Trojan to his gilded bark
With fond reluctance, yielding modesty,
And oft reverted eye, as if she knew not
Whether she fear'd, or wish'd to be pursued.

SONNET

On the Death of

Mr. Richard West

In vain to me the smiling Mornings shine,
And redd'ning Phœbus lifts his golden fire:
The Birds in vain their amorous Descant join;
Or chearful fields resume their green attire:
These ears, alas! for other notes repine,   *5*
A different Object do these eyes require.
My lonely anguish melts no heart but mine;
And in my breast the imperfect joys expire.
Yet Morning smiles the busy Race to chear,
And new-born pleasure brings to happier men: *10*
The fields to all their wonted tribute bear:
To warm their little loves the birds complain:
I fruitless mourn to him, that cannot hear,
And weep the more, because I weep in vain.

Hymn to Ignorance

A Fragment

Hail, Horrors, hail! ye ever-gloomy bowers,
Ye gothic fanes, and antiquated towers,
Where rushy Camus' slowly-winding flood
Perpetual draws his humid train of mud:
Glad I revisit thy neglected reign,   *5*
Oh, take me to thy peaceful shade again.
    But chiefly thee, whose influence breath'd from high

Augments the native darkness of the sky;
Ah, Ignorance! soft salutary Power!
Prostrate with filial reverence I adore.   *10*
Thrice hath Hyperion roll'd his annual race,
Since weeping I forsook thy fond embrace.
Oh say, successful do'st thou still oppose
Thy leaden Ægis 'gainst our antient foes?
Still stretch, tenacious of thy right divine,   *15*
The massy sceptre o'er thy slumb'ring line?
And dews Lethean thro' the land dispense
To steep in slumbers each benighted sense?
If any spark of Wit's delusive ray
Break out, and flash a momentary day,   *20*
With damp, cold touch forbid it to aspire,
And huddle up in fogs the dangerous fire.
     Oh say—she hears me not, but, careless grown,
Lethargic nods upon her ebon throne.
Goddess! awake, arise! alas my fears!   *25*
Can powers immortal feel the force of years?
Not thus of old, with ensigns wide unfurl'd,
She rode triumphant o'er the vanquish'd world;
Fierce nations own'd her unresisted might,
And all was Ignorance, and all was Night.   *30*
     Oh! sacred Age! Oh Times for ever lost!
(The School-man's glory, and the Church-man's boast.)
For ever gone—yet still to Fancy new,
Her rapid wings the transient scene pursue,
And bring the buried ages back to view.   *35*
     High on her car, behold the Grandam ride
Like old Sesostris with barbaric pride;
......a team of harness'd monarchs bend......

THE ALLIANCE OF EDUCATION
AND GOVERNMENT

A FRAGMENT

Essay I.

...πόταγ᾽, ὦ ᾽γαθέ· τὰν γὰρ ἀοιδάν
οὔτι πω εἰς Ἀΐδαν γε τὸν ἐκλελάθοντα φυλαξεῖς.
     —Theocritus, *Idyll* i. 62-63].

As sickly Plants betray a niggard Earth,
  Whose barren Bosom starves her gen'rous Birth,
Nor genial Warmth nor genial Juice retains
Their Roots to feed, and fill their verdant Veins:
And as in Climes, where Winter holds his Reign,   *5*
The Soil, tho' fertile, will not teem in vain,
Forbids her Gems to swell, her Shades to rise,
Nor trusts her Blossoms to the churlish Skies.
So draw Mankind in vain the vital Airs,
Unform'd, unfriended, by those kindly Cares   *10*
That Health and Vigour to the Soul impart,
Spread the young Thought, and warm the opening Heart.
So fond Instruction on the growing Powers
Of Nature idly lavishes her Stores,
If equal Justice with unclouded Face   *15*
Smile not indulgent on the rising Race,
And scatter with a free tho' frugal Hand
Light golden Showers of Plenty o'er the Land:
But Tyranny has fix'd her Empire there,
To check their tender Hopes with chilling Fear,   *20*
And blast the blooming Promise of the Year.
  This spacious animated Scene survey
From where the rolling Orb, that gives the Day,
His sable Sons with nearer Course surrounds,

To either Pole, and Life's remotest Bounds.   *25*
How rude so e'er th' exterior Form we find,
Howe'er Opinion tinge the varied Mind,
Alike to all the Kind impartial Heav'n
The Sparks of Truth and Happiness has given:
With Sense to feel, with Mem'ry to retain,   *30*
They follow Pleasure and they fly from Pain;
Their Judgement mends the Plan their Fancy draws,
Th' Event presages, and explores the Cause.
The soft Returns of Gratitude they know,
By Fraud elude, by Force repel the Foe;   *35*
While mutual Wishes, mutual Woes, endear
The social Smile and sympathetic Tear.
    Say then, thro' Ages by what Fate confined
To different Climes seem different Souls assign'd?
Here measured Laws and philosophic Ease   *40*
Fix, and improve the polish'd Arts of Peace.
There Industry and Gain their Vigils keep,
Command the Winds, and tame th' unwilling Deep.
Here Force and hardy Deeds of Blood prevail;
There languid Pleasure sighs in every Gale.   *45*
Oft o'er the trembling Nations from afar
Has Scythia breath'd the living Cloud of War;
And, where the deluge burst, with sweepy Sway
Their Arms, their Kings, their Gods were roll'd away.
As oft have issued, Host impelling Host,   *50*
The blue-eyed Myriads from the Baltic Coast.
The prostrate South to the Destroyer yields
Her boasted Titles and her golden Fields:
With grim Delight the Brood of Winter view
A brighter Day, and heavens of azure Hue,   *55*
Scent the new Fragrance of the breathing Rose,
And quaff the pendent Vintage, as it grows.
Proud of the yoke, and pliant to the Rod,
Why yet does Asia dread a Monarch's nod,
While European Freedom still withstands   *60*
Th' encroaching tide, that drowns her less'ning Lands,

And sees far off with an indignant groan
Her native Plains, and Empires once her own?
Can opener Skies, and Suns of fiercer Flame
O'erpower the Fire that animates our Frame;   65
As Lamps, that shed at Ev'n a chearful Ray,
Fade and expire beneath the Eye of Day?
Need we the influence of the Northern Star
To string our Nerves and steel our Hearts to War?
And, where the Face of Nature laughs around,   70
Must sick'ning Virtue fly the tainted Ground?
Unmanly Thought! what Seasons can controul,
What fancied Zone can circumscribe the Soul,
Who, conscious of the Source from whence she springs,
By Reason's light on Resolution's wings,   75
Spite of her frail Companion, dauntless goes
O'er Libya's Deserts and thro' Zembla's snows?
She bids each slumb'ring Energy awake,
Another Touch, another Temper take,
Suspends th' inferiour Laws that rule our Clay: 80
The stubborn Elements confess her Sway;
Their little Wants, their low Desires, refine,
And raise the Mortal to a Height divine.
   Not but the human Fabrick from the Birth
Imbibes a flavour of its parent Earth: 85
As various Tracts enforce a various Toil.
The Manners speak the Idiom of their Soil.
An Iron-Race the Mountain-Cliffs maintain,
Foes to the gentler Genius of the Plain:
For where unwearied Sinews must be found   90
With sidelong Plough to quell the flinty Ground,
To turn the Torrent's swift-descending Flood,
To brave the Savage rushing from the Wood,
What wonder, if to patient Valour train'd
They guard with Spirit, what by Strength they gain'd?   95
And while their rocky Ramparts round they see,
The rough abode of want and liberty,
(As lawless Force from Confidence will grow)

Insult the Plenty of the Vales below?
What wonder in the sultry Climes, that spread,   *100*
Where Nile redundant o'er his summer-bed
From his broad bosom life and verdure flings,
And broods o'er Egypt with his wat'ry wings,
If with advent'rous oar and ready sail,
The dusky people drive before the gale: *105*
Or on frail floats to distant cities ride,
That rise and glitter o'er the ambient tide.

Stanzas to Mr. Bentley

In silent gaze the tuneful choir among,
    Half pleas'd, half blushing, let the Muse admire,
While Bentley leads her sister-art along,
    And bids the pencil answer to the lyre.

See, in their course, each transitory thought   *5*
    Fix'd by his touch a lasting essence take;
Each dream, in fancy's airy colouring wrought,
    To local Symmetry and life awake!

The tardy rhymes that us'd to linger on,
    To censure cold, and negligent of fame,   *10*
In swifter measures animated run,
    And catch a lustre from his genuine flame.

Ah! could they catch his strength, his easy grace,
    His quick creation, his unerring line;
The energy of Pope they might efface,   *15*
    And Dryden's harmony submit to mine.

But not to one in this benighted age
    Is that diviner inspiration giv'n,
That burns in Shakespear's or in Milton's page,
    The pomp and prodigality of heav'n.   *20*

As, when conspiring in the diamond's blaze,
    The meaner gems, that singly charm the sight,
Together dart their intermingled rays,
    And dazzle with a luxury of light.

Enough for me, if to some feeling breast   *25*
    My lines a secret sympathy …
And as their pleasing influence …
    A sigh of soft reflection …

ODE

On the Pleasure arising from Vicissitude

Now the golden Morn aloft
    Waves her dew-bespangled wing;
With vermil cheek, and whisper soft
    She wooes the tardy Spring:
Till April starts, and calls around   5
The sleeping fragrance from the ground;
And lightly o'er the living scene
Scatters his freshest, tenderest green.

New-born flocks, in rustic dance,
    Frisking ply their feeble feet;   10
Forgetful of their wintry trance
    The Birds his presence greet:
But chief, the Sky-lark warbles high
His trembling thrilling ecstasy
And, less'ning from the dazzled sight,   15
Melts into air and liquid light.

[Rise, my soul! on wings of fire,
    Rise the rapt'rous Choir among;
Hark! 'tis Nature strikes the Lyre,
    And leads the general song:]   20

Yesterday the sullen year
    Saw the snowy whirlwind fly;
Mute was the music of the air,
    The Herd stood drooping by:
Their raptures now that wildly flow,   25
No yesterday, nor morrow know;
'Tis Man alone that joy descries
With forward, and reverted eyes.

Smiles on past Misfortune's brow
    Soft Reflection's hand can trace;   *30*
And o'er the cheek of Sorrow throw
    A melancholy grace;
While Hope prolongs our happier hour,
Or deepest shades, that dimly lower
And blacken round our weary way,   *35*
Gilds with a gleam of distant day.

Still, where rosy Pleasure leads,
    See a kindred Grief pursue;
Behind the steps that Misery treads,
    Approaching Comfort view: *40*
The hues of Bliss more brightly glow,
Chastised by sabler tints of woe;
And blended form, with artful strife,
The strength and harmony of Life.

See the Wretch, that long has tost   *45*
    On the thorny bed of Pain,
At length repair his vigour lost,
    And breathe and walk again:
The meanest flowret of the vale,
The simplest note that swells the gale,   *50*
The common Sun, the air, the skies,
To Him are opening Paradise.

Humble Quiet builds her cell
    Near the source whence Pleasure flows;
She eyes the clear chrystalline well,   *55*
    And tastes it as it goes.
Far below,   the crowd.

Broad and turbulent it grows

       With restless sweep
They perish in the boundless deep.   *60*

Mark where Indolence, and Pride,
Softly rolling, side by side,
Their dull, but daily round.

[Poem left incomplete]

Epitaph on Mrs Clerke

Lo! where this silent Marble weeps,
A Friend, a Wife, a Mother sleeps:
A Heart, within whose sacred cell
The peaceful Virtues lov'd to dwell:
Affection warm, and faith sincere,   5
And soft humanity were there.
In agony, in death resign'd,
She felt the Wound she left behind.
Her infant Image, here below,
Sits smiling on a Father's woe: 10
Whom what awaits, while yet he strays
Along the lonely vale of days?
A Pang, to secret sorrow dear;
A Sigh; an unavailing Tear;
'Till time shall ev'ry grief remove,   15
With Life, with Memory, and with Love.

Epitaph on a Child

Here, freed from pain, secure from misery, lies
    A child, the darling of his parents' eyes:
A gentler lamb ne'er sported on the plain,
A fairer flower will never bloom again.
Few were the days allotted to his breath;   5
Now let him sleep in peace his night of death.

Epitaph on Mrs Mason

Tell them, though 'tis an awful thing to die,
    ('Twas ev'n to thee) yet the dread path once trod,
Heaven lifts its everlasting portals high,
And bids "the pure in heart behold their God."

Epitaph on Sir William Williams

Here, foremost in the dangerous paths of fame,
    Young Williams fought for England's fair renown;
His mind each muse, each grace adorn'd his frame,
    Nor Envy dared to view him with a frown.
At Aix his voluntary sword he drew,   5
    There first in blood his infant honor seal'd;
From fortune, pleasure, science, love he flew,
    And scorn'd repose when Britain took the field.
With eyes of flame, and cool undaunted breast,
    Victor he stood on Bellisle's rocky steeps—   10
Ah! gallant Youth! this marble tells the rest,
    Where melancholy Friendship bends and weeps.

[Sketch of His Own Character]

Too poor for a bribe and too proud to importune,
   He had not the method of making a fortune:
Could love and could hate, so was thought somewhat odd;
No very great wit, he believed in a God.
A post or a pension he did not desire,   5
But left church and state to Charles Townshend and Squire.

[The Death of Hoel]

From Aneurin, Monarch of the Bards.
extracted from the Gododin

Had I but the torrent's might,
   With headlong rage and wild affright
Upon Deïra's squadrons hurl'd,
To rush, and sweep them from the world!

   Too, too secure in youthful pride,   5
By them my friend, my Hoel, died,
Great Cian's son: of Madoc old
He ask'd no heaps of hoarded gold;
Alone in nature's wealth array'd,
He ask'd and had the lovely Maid.   10
   To Cattraeth's vale in glitt'ring row
Twice two hundred Warriors go;
Every Warrior's manly neck
Chains of regal honour deck,
Wreath'd in many a golden link: 15
From the golden cup they drink

Nectar, that the bees produce,
Or the grape's extatic juice.
Flush'd with mirth, and hope they burn:
But none from Cattraeth's vale return,   *20*
Save Aëron brave, and Conan strong,
(Bursting thro' the bloody throng)
And I, the meanest of them all,
That live to weep, and sing their fall.

[CARADOC]

Have ye seen the tusky Boar,
Or the Bull, with sullen roar,
On surrounding Foes advance?
So Caradoc bore his lance.

[CONAN]

Conan's name, my lay, rehearse,
Build to him the lofty verse,
Sacred tribute of the Bard,
Verse, the Hero's sole reward.
As the flame's devouring force;   *5*
As the whirlwind in its course;
As the thunder's fiery stroke,
Glancing on the shiver'd oak;
Did the sword of Conan mow
The crimson harvest of the foe.   *10*

THE CANDIDATE

When sly Jemmy Twitcher had smugg'd up his face
    With a lick of court white-wash, and pious grimace,
A wooing he went, where three Sisters of old
In harmless society guttle and scold.
    Lord! Sister, says Physic to Law, I declare   5
Such a sheep-biting look, such a pick-pocket air,
Not I, for the Indies! you know I'm no prude;
But his nose is a shame and his eyes are so lewd!
Then he shambles and straddles so oddly, I fear—
No; at our time of life, 'twould be silly, my dear."   10
    I don't know, says Law, now methinks, for his look,
'Tis just like the picture in Rochester's book.
But his character, Phyzzy, his morals, his life;
When she died, I can't tell, but he once had a wife.
    They say he's no Christian, loves drinking and whoring, 15
And all the town rings of his swearing and roaring,
His lying and filching, and Newgate-bird tricks:—
Not I,—for a coronet, chariot and six.
    Divinity heard, between waking and dozing,
Her sisters denying, and Jemmy proposing;   20
From dinner she rose with her bumper in hand,
She stroked up her belly, and stroked down her band.
    What a pother is here about wenching and roaring!
Why David loved catches, and Solomon whoring.
Did not Israel filch from th' Ægyptians of old   25
Their jewels of silver, and jewels of gold?
The prophet of Bethel, we read, told a lie:
He drinks; so did Noah; he swears; so do I.
To refuse him for such peccadillos, were odd;
Besides, he repents, and he talks about G—.   30
    Never hang down your head, you poor penitent elf!
Come, buss me, I'll be Mrs Twitcher myself.
D—n ye both for a couple of Puritan bitches!
He's Christian enough, that repents and, that [stitches]."

Verses from Shakespeare

WILLIAM SHAKESPEARE to Mrs ANNE, Regular Servant
to the Revd Mr PRECENTOR of York.

A moment's patience, gentle Mistris Anne!
   (But stint your clack for sweet St. Charitie)
'Tis Willy begs, once a right proper man,
Tho' now a book, and interleav'd, you see.
   Much have I born from canker'd Critick's spite,   5
From fumbling Baronets, and Poets small,
Pert Barristers, & Parsons nothing bright:
But, what awaits me now, is worst of all!
   'Tis true, our master's temper natural
Was fashion'd fair in meek & dove-like guise;   10
But may not honey's self be turn'd to gall
By residence, by marriage, & sore eyes?
   If then he wreak on me his wicked will,
Steal to his closet at the hour of prayer;
And (when thou hear'st the organ piping shrill)   15
Grease his best pen, and all he scribbles, tear.
Better to bottom tarts & cheesecakes nice,
   Better the roast-meat from the fire to save,
Better be twisted into caps for spice,
Than thus be patch'd & cobbled in one's grave.   20
   So York shall taste what Clouët never knew;
So from *our* works sublimer fumes shall rise:
While Nancy earns the praise to Shakespear due
For glorious puddings, & immortal pies.

[Song I]

'MIDST beauty and pleasure's gay triumphs, to languish
    And droop without knowing the source of my anguish:
To start from short slumbers and look for the morning—
Yet close my dull eyes when I see it returning;

Sighs sudden and frequent, looks ever dejected
Sounds that steal from my tongue, by no meaning connected!
Ah say, fellow-swains, how these symptoms befell me?
They smile, but reply not. Sure Delia will tell me!

[Song II]

Thyrsis, when we parted, swore
    Ere the spring he would return.
Ah, what means yon violet flower,
And the buds that deck the thorn?
'Twas the Lark that upward sprung!   5
'Twas the Nightingale that sung!

Idle notes, untimely green,
Why such unavailing haste?
Western gales and skies serene
Prove not always winter past.   10
Cease my doubts, my fears to move;
Spare the honour of my love.

SATIRE ON THE HEADS OF HOUSES

OR, NEVER A BARREL THE BETTER HERRING

O Cambridge, attend
To the satire I've pen'd
On the Heads of thy Houses,
Thou Seat of the Muses!

Know the Master of Jesus   5
Does hugely displease us;
The Master of Maudlin
In the same dirt is dawdling;
The Master of Sidney
Is of the same kidney;   10
The Master of Trinity
To him bears affinity;
As the Master of Keys
Is as like as two pease,
So the Master of Queen's   15
Is as like as two beans;
The Master of King's
Copies them in all things;
The Master of Catherine
Takes them all for his pattern;   20
The Master of Clare
Hits them all to a hair;
The Master of Christ
By the rest is enticed;
But the Master of Emmanuel   25
Follows them like a spaniel;
The Master of Benet
Is of the like tenet;
The Master of Pembroke
Has from them his system took;   30
The Master of Peter's

Has all the same features;
The Master of St John's
Like the rest of the dons.

P.S. —As to Trinity Hall   *35*
We say nothing at all.

[Tophet]

Inscription on a portrait.

Such Tophet was; so looked the grinning fiend
   Whom many a frighted prelates called his friend;
I saw them bow and, while they wished him dead,
With servile simper nod the mitred head.
Our Mother-Church with half-averted sight   *5*
Blush'd as she blessed her grisly proselyte:
Hosannahs rung through Hell's tremendous borders,
And Satan's self had thoughts of taking orders.

[INVITATION TO MASON]

Prim Hurd attends your call, and Palgrave proud,
Stonhewer the lewd, and Delaval the loud.
For thee does Powell squeeze, and Marriot sputter,
And Glyn cut phizzes, & Tom Neville stutter.
Brown sees thee sitting on his nose's tip,   5
The Widow feels thee in her aching hip,
For thee fat Nanny sighs, and handy Nelly,
And Balguy with a bishop in his belly!

[COUPLET ABOUT BIRDS]

There pipes the woodlark, and the song-thrush there
Scatters his loose notes in the waste of air.

[PARODY ON AN EPITAPH]

Now clean, now hideous, mellow now, now gruff,
She swept, she hiss'd, she ripen'd and grew rough,
At Broom, Pendragon, Appleby & Brough.

[IMPROMPTUS]

EXTEMPORE BY MR. GR[AY]. ON DR. K[EENE].
B[ISHOP]. OF C[HESTER].

The Bishop of Chester
Though wiser than Nestor
And fairer than Esther,
If you scratch him will fester.

ONE DAY THE BISHOP HAVING OFFERED TO GIVE A
GENTLEMAN A GOOSE MR. GR[AY] COMPOSED
HIS EPITAPH, THUS.

Here lies Edmund Keene Lord Bishop of Chester,
He eat a fat goose, and could not digest her—

AND THIS UPON HIS LADY—

Here lies Mrs Keene the Bishop of Chester,
She had a bad face which did sadly molest her.

IMPROMPTU BY MR. GRAY GOING OUT OF RABY CASTLE

Here lives Harry Vane,
Very good claret and fine champagne.

A COUPLET BY MR. GRAY

When you rise from your dinner as light as before,
'Tis a sign you have eat just enough and no more.

[Lines on Dr Robert Smith]

Do you ask why old Focus Silvanus defies,
  And leaves not a chestnut in being?
'Tis not that old Focus himself has got eyes,
But because he has writ about seeing.

Lines written at Burnham

And, as they bow their hoary Tops, relate
  In murm'ring Sounds the dark Decrees of Fate;
While Visions, as Poetic eyes avow,
Cling to each Leaf and swarm on ev'ry Bough:

Lines on the Accession of George III

The Old One's dead,
  And in his stead,
    The New One takes his place;
The sing and sigh,4
And laugh and cry,
    With dismal cheerful face.

[Lines Spoken by the Ghost of John Dennis at the Devil Tavern]

From purling Streams & the Elysian Scene,
From Groves, that smile with never-fading Green
I reascend: in Atropos' despight
Restored to Celadon, & upper light:
Ye gods, that sway the Regions under ground,   5
Reveal to mortal View your realms profound;
At his command admit the eye of Day;
When Celadon commands, what God can disobey?
Nor seeks he your Tartarean fires to know,
The house of Torture and th' Abyss of Woe;   10
But happy fields and Mansions free from Pain,
Gay Meads, and springing flowers, best please yᵉ gentle Swain:
   That little, naked, melancholy thing
My Soul, when first she tryed her flight to wing;
Began with speed new Regions to explore,   15
And blunder'd thro' a narrow Postern door;
First most devoutly having said its Prayers,
It tumbled down a thousand pair of [Stairs],
Thro' Entries long, thro' Cellars vast & deep,
Where ghostly Rats their habitations keep,
Where Spiders spread their Webs, & owlish Goblins sleep. 20
After so many Chances had befell,
It came into a mead of Asphodel:
Betwixt the Confines of yᵉ light and dark
It lies, of 'Lyzium yᵉ St. James's park:
Here Spirit-Beaux flutter along the Mall,   25
And Shadows in disguise scate o'er yᵉ Iced Canal;
Here groves embower'd, & more sequester'd Shades,
Frequented by yᵉ Ghosts of Ancient Maids,
Are seen to rise: the melancholy Scene,
With gloomy haunts, & twilight walks between   30
Conceals the wayward band: here spend their time

Greensickness Girls, that died in youthful prime,
Virgins forlorn, all dressed in Willow-green-i
With Queen Elizabeth and Nicolini.
    More to reveal, or many words to use   *35*
Would tire alike your patience & my muse.
Believe, that never was so faithful found
Queen Proserpine to Pluto under ground,
Or Cleopatra to her Marc-Antony,
As Orozmades to his Celadony.   *40*
        P.S.
Lucrece for half a crown will shew you fun,
But Mrs Oldfield is become a Nun.
Nobles and Cits, Prince Pluto and his Spouse
Flock to the Ghost of Covent-Garden house:
Plays, which were hiss'd above, below revive;   *45*
When dead applauded, that were damn'd alive:
The People, as in life, still keep their Passions,
But differ something from the world in Fashions.
Queen Artemisia breakfasts on Bohea,
And Alexander wears a Ramilie.   *50*

THE CHARACTERS OF THE CHRIST-CROSS ROW, BY A CRITIC, TO MRS——

Great D draws near—the Duchess sure is come,
Open the doors of the withdrawing-room:
Her daughters decked most daintily I see,
The Dowager grows a perfect double D.
E enters next and with her Eve appears,   5
Not like yon dowager depressed with years;
What ease and elegance her person grace,
Bright beaming, as the evening-star, her face.
Queen Esther next—how fair e'en after death;
Then one faint glimpse of Queen Elizabeth;   10
No more, our Esthers now are nought but Hetties,
Elizabeths all dwindled into Betties.
In vain you think to find them under E,
They're all diverted into H and B.
F follows fast the fair—and in his rear,   15
See folly, fashion, foppery straight appear,
All with fantastic clews, fantastic clothes,
With fans and flounces, fringe and furbelows.
Here Grub-street geese presume to joke and jeer,
All, all but Grannam Osborne's *Gazetteer*.   20
High heaves his hugeness H, methinks we see,
Henry the Eighth's most monstrous majesty,
But why on such *mock* grandeur should we dwell,
H mounts to heaven and H descends to hell.
As H the Hebrew found, so I the Jew: 25
See Isaac, Joseph, Jacob pass in view;
The walls of old Jerusalem appear,
See Israel and all Judah thronging there.

* * * *

P pokes his head out, yet has not a pain;
Like Punch he peeps, but soon pops in again.   30
Pleased with his pranks, the pisgys calls him Puck,

Mortals he loves to prick, and pinch, and pluck.
Now a pert prig, he perks upon your face;
Now peers, pores, ponders, with profound grimace;
Now a proud prince, in pompous purple dressed,   35
And now a player, a peer, a pimp or priest,
A pea, a pin, in a perpetual round,
Now seems a penny, and now shews a Pound;
Like perch or pike, in pond you see him come;
He in plantations hangs like pear or plum,   40
Pippin or peach; then perches on the spray,
In form of parrot, pye or popinjay.
P, Proteus-like, all tricks, all shapes can shew,
The pleasantest person in the Christ-Cross Row.

* * * *

As K a king, Q represents a queen,   45
And seems small difference the sounds between.
K as a man with hoarser accent speaks;
In shriller notes Q like a female squeaks.
Behold K struts as might a King become;
Q draws her train along the drawing-room.   50
Slow follow all the quality of state:
Queer Queensberry only does refuse to wait. [...]

* * * *

Thus great R reigns in town, while different far,
Rests in retirement *little* rural R;
Remote from cities lives in lone retreat,   55
With rooks and rabbit burrows round his seat—
S, sails the Swan slow down the silver stream. [...]

* * * *

So, big with weddings, waddles W,
And brings all womankind before your view:
A wench, a wife, a widow and a w[hor]e,   60
With woe behind, and wantonness before.

Verse Fragments

Gratitude
    The Joy that trembles in her eye
    She bows her meek & humble head
              [...] in silent praise
          [...] beyond the power of Sound.

* * * *

(Mr Pope dead)
    [...] and smart beneath the visionary scourge
    —'tis Ridicule & not reproach that wounds
    Their vanity & not their conscience feels
    [...]
             a few shall [...]
    The cadence of my song repeat
    and hail thee in my words.

TRANSLATIONS

Translation from Dante, *Inferno* Canto XXXIII 1-78

From his dire Food the griesly Fellon raised
His Gore-dyed Lips, which on the clotter'd Locks
Of th' half-devoured Head he wiped, & thus
Began: Would'st thou revive the deep Despair,
The Anguish, that, unutter'd, natheless wrings   5
My inmost Heart? yet if the telling may
Beget the Traitour's Infamy, whom thus
I ceaseless gnaw insatiate; thou shalt see me
At once give loose to Utterance and to Tears.

I know not, who thou art; nor on what Errand   10
Sent hither; but a Florentine my Ear,
Won by thy Tongue, declares thee. Know, thou see'st
In me Count Ugolino, and Ruggieri,
Pisa's perfidious Prelate, this: now hear
My Wrongs and from them judge of my Revenge.   15

That I did trust him, that I was betray'd
By trusting, and by Treachery slain, it rekes not
That I advise thee; that which yet remains
To thee and all unknown (a horrid Tale),
The Bitterness of Death, I shall unfold.   20
Attend, and say if he have injured me.

Thro' a small crevice opening, what scant light
That grim and antique Tower admitted (since
Of me the Tower of Famine hight, and known
To many a wretch) already 'gan the dawn   25
To send: the whilst I slumbering lay, a Sleep
Prophetic of my Woes with direful Hand
Oped the dark Veil of Fate. I saw methought
Toward Pisa's Mount, that intercepts the View
Of Lucca, chas'd by hell-hounds gaunt and bloody   30

A Wolf full-grown; with fleet and equal Speed
His young ones ran beside him. Lanfranc there
And Sigismundo, and Gualandi rode
Amain, my deadly foes, headed by this
The deadliest: He their chief, the foremost he   35
Flash'd to pursue and chear the eager Cry.
Nor long endur'd the Chase: the panting Sire,
Of Strength bereft, his helpless offspring soon
O'erta'en beheld, and in their trembling Flanks
The hungry Pack their sharp-set Fangs embrued.   40

The Morn had scarce commenc'd, when I awoke:
My children (they were with me) sleep as yet
Gave not to know their Sum of Misery,
But yet in low and uncompleated Sounds
I heard 'em wail for Bread. Oh! thou art cruel,   45
Or thou dost mourn to think, what my poor Heart
Foresaw, foreknew: oh! if thou weep not now,
Where are thy Tears? too soon they had aroused 'em,
Sad with the Fears of Sleep, and now the Hour
Of timely Food approach'd; when, at the Gate   50
Below I heard the dreadful Clash of Bars
And fastening Bolts: then on my Children's Eyes
Speechless my Sight I fix'd, nor wept, for all
Within was Stone: they wept, unhappy Boys!
They wept, and first my little dear Anselmo   55
Cried, Father, why do you gaze so sternly?
What would you have? Yet wept I not or answer'd
All that whole day or the succeeding Night,
Till a new Sun arose with weakly Gleam
And wan, such as mought entrance find within   60
That House of Woe. But oh! when I beheld
My Sons, and in four Faces saw my own
Despair reflected, either hand I gnaw'd
For Anguish, which they construed hunger; straight
Ariseing all they cried, far less shall be   65
Our Suffering, sir, if you resume your Gift;

These miserable Limbs with Flesh you cloath'd;
Take back, what once was yours. I swallowed down
My struggling Sorrow, nor to heighten theirs:
That day, and yet another, mute we sate.   *70*
And motionless; oh Earth, could'st thou not gape
Quick to devour me? yet a fourth Day came,
When Gaddo, at my Feet outstretch'd, imploreing
In vain my Help, expir'd; ere the sixth Morn
Had dawn'd, my other three before my Eyes   *75*
Died one by one; I saw 'em fall; I heard
Their doleful Cries; for three days more I grop'd
About among their cold Remains (for then
Hunger had reft my Eye-sight), often calling
On their dear Names, that heard me now no more: *80*
The fourth, what Sorrow could not, famine did.

He finished: Then with unrelenting Eye
Askaunce he turn'd him, hasty to renew
The hellish Feast, and rent his trembling Prey.

Translation from Statius,
Thebaid VI 646-88, 704-24

E Lib: 6to Thebaidos

Then thus the king: Whoe'er the quoit can wield,
And furthest send its weight athwart the field,
Let him stand forth his brawny arm to boast.
Swift at the word, from out the gazing host,   *5*
Young Pterelas with strength unequal drew,
Labouring the disc, and to small distance threw.
The band around admire the mighty mass,
A slippery weight and formed of polished brass.
The love of honour bade two youths advance,   *10*
Achaians born, to try the glorious chance;
A third arose, of Acarnania he,
Of Pisa one and three from Ephyre.
Nor more; for now Nesimachus's son,
By acclamations roused, came towering on.   *15*
Another orb upheaved his strong right hand,
Then thus: "Ye Argive flower, ye warlike band,
Who trust your arms shall raze the Tyrian towers,
And batter Cadmus' walls with stony showers,
Receive a worthier load; yon puny ball   *20*
Let youngsters toss."
He said, and scornful flung the unheeded weight
Aloof: the champions trembling at the sight
Prevent disgrace, the palm despaired resign.
All but two youths the enormous orb decline: *25*
These conscious shame witheld and pride of noble line.
As bright and huge the spacious circle lay,
With doubled light it beamed against the day:
So glittering shows the Thracian godhead's shield,
With such a gleam affrights Pangaea's field,   *30*
When blazing 'gainst the sun it shines from far,
And, clashed, rebellows with the din of war.

Phlegyas the long-expected play began.
Summoned his strength and call'd forth all the man.
All eyes were bent on his experienced hand,   *35*
For oft in Pisa's sports his native land
Admired that arm; oft on Alpheus' shore
The ponderous brass in exercise he bore;
Where flow'd the widest stream he took his stand;
Sure flew the disc from his unerring hand.   *40*
Nor stopp'd till it had cut the further strand.
And now in dust the polish'd ball he roll'd,
Then grasp'd its weight, elusive of his hold;
Now fitting to his grip and nervous arm.
Suspends the crowd with animation warm;   *45*
Nor tempts he yet the plain but, hurl'd upright.
Emits the mass, a prelude of his might;
Firmly he plants each knee and o'er his head.
Collecting all his force, the circle sped;
It towers to cut the clouds; now through the skies   *50*
Sings in its rapid way and strengthens as it flies;
Anon with slackened rage comes quivering down,
Heavy and huge, and cleaves the solid ground.

So from the astonished stars, her nightly train,
The sun's pale sister, drawn by magic strain,   *55*
Deserts precipitant her darken'd sphere:
In vain the nations with officious fear
Their cymbals toss and sounding brass explore;
Th' Æmonian hag enjoys her dreadful hour.
And smiles malignant on the labouring power.   *60*

* * *

Third in the labours of the Disc came on,
With sturdy step and slow, Hippomedon;
Artful and strong he pois'd the well-known weight
By Phlegyas warn'd and fir'd by Mnestheus' fate,
That to avoid, and this to emulate.   *65*

His vigorous arm he try'd before he flung,
Brac'd all his nerves and every sinew strung;
Then with a tempest's whirl and wary eye,
Pursu'd his cast and hurl'd the orb on high;
The orb on high tenacious of its course.   70
True to the mighty arm that gave it force,
Far overleaps all bound, and joys to see
Its antient lord secure of victory.
The theatre's green height and woody wall
Tremble ere it precipitates its fall,   75
The ponderous mass sinks in the cleaving ground,
While vales and woods and echoing hills rebound.
As when from Ætna's smoking summit broke,
The eyeless Cyclops heav'd the craggy rock;
Where Ocean frets beneath the dashing oar,   80
And parting surges round the vessel roar;
'Twas there he aim'd the meditated harm,
And scarce Ulysses scap'd his giant arm.
A tyger's pride the victor bore away,
With native spots and artful labour gay,   85
A shining border round the margin roll'd,
And calm'd the terrors of his claws in gold.

TRANSLATION FROM STATIUS,
Thebaid IX 319-26

Crenaeus, whom the nymph Ismenis bore
To Faunus on the Theban river's shore,
With new-born heat amidst his native stream
Exults in arms, which cast an iron gleam.
In this clear wave he first beheld the day;   *5*
On the green bank first taught his steps to stray,
To skim the parent flood and on the margin play:
Fear he disdains and scorns the power of fate,
Secure within his mother's wat'ry state.
The youth exulting stems the bloody tide,   *10*
Visits each bank and stalks with martial pride,
While old Ismenus' gently-rolling wave
Delights the favourite youth within its flood to lave.
Whether the youth obliquely steers his course
Or cuts the downward stream with equal force,   *15*
The indulgent river strives his steps to aid.

Translation from Tasso
Gerusalemme Liberata Canto 14, St. 32.

Preser commiato: e si 'l desio gli sprona, &c:

Dismissed at length, they break through all delay
To tempt the dangers of the doubtful way;
And first to Ascalon their steps they bend,
Whose walls along the neighbouring sea extend,
Nor yet in prospect rose the distant shore;   *5*
Scarce the hoarse waves from far were heard to roar,
When thwart the road a river rolled its flood
Tempestuous, and all further course withstood;
The torrent stream his ancient bounds disdains,
Swoll'n with new force, and late-descending rains.   *10*
Irresolute they stand; when lo, appears
The wondrous Sage: vigorous he seem'd in years,
Awful his mien, low as his feet there flows
A vestment unadorn'd, though white as new-fall'n snows;
Against the stream the waves secure he trod.   *15*
His head a chaplet bore, his hand a rod.
   As on the Rhine when Boreas' fury reigns,
And winter binds the floods in icy chains,
Swift shoots the village-maid in rustick play
Smooth, without step, adown the shining way,   *20*
Fearless in long excursion loves to glide,
And sports and wantons o'er the frozen tide.
   So moved the Seer, but on no harden'd plain;
The river boiled beneath, and rushed towards the main.
Where fix'd in wonder stood the warlike pair,   *25*
His course he turn'd and thus relieved their care:
   "Vast, oh my friends, and difficult the toil
To seek your hero in a distant soil!
No common helps, no common guide ye need,
Art it requires, and more than winged speed.   *30*
What length of sea remains, what various lands,
Oceans unknown, inhospitable sands!

For adverse fate the captive chief has hurl'd
Beyond the confines of our narrow world:
Great things and full of wonder in your ears   *35*
I shall unfold; but first dismiss your fears;
Nor doubt with me to tread the downward road
That to the grotto leads, my dark abode."
     Scarce had he said, before the warriors' eyes
When mountain-high the waves disparted rise;   *40*
The flood on either hand its billows rears,
And in the midst a spacious arch appears.
Their hands he seized, and down the steep he led
Beneath the obedient river's inmost bed;
The watery glimmerings of a fainter day   *45*
Discovered half, and half concealed their way;
As when athwart the dusky woods by night
The uncertain crescent gleams a sickly light.
Through subterraneous passages they went,
Earth's inmost cells, and caves of deep descent;   *50*
Of many a flood they viewed the secret source,
The birth of rivers, rising to their course,
Whate'er with copious train its channel fills,
Floats into lakes, and bubbles into rills;
The Po was there to see, Danubius' bed,   *55*
Euphrates' font, and Nile's mysterious head.
Further they pass, where ripening minerals flow,
And embryon metals undigested glow,
Sulphureous veins and living silver shine,
Which soon the parent sun's warm powers refine.   *60*
In one rich mass unite the precious store,
The parts combine and harden into ore:
Here gems break through the night with glittering beam,
And paint the margin of the costly stream,
All stones of lustre shoot their vivid ray,   *65*
And mix attempered in a various day;
Here the soft emerald smiles of verdant hue,
And rubies flame, with sapphire's heavenly blue,
The diamond there attracts the wondrous sight,
Proud of its thousand dies and luxury of light.   *70*

IMITATED FROM *Propertius*. Lib: 2: Eleg: 1.

To Mæcenas.

You ask, why thus my Loves I still rehearse.
   Whence the soft Strain and ever-melting verse:
From Cynthia all that in my numbers shines;
She is my genius, she inspires the Lines;
No Phœbus else, no other Muse I know;   *5*
She tunes my easy Rhime, and gives the Lay to flow.
If the loose Curls around her Forehead play.
Or lawless, o'er their Ivory Margin stray:
If the thin Coan Web her Shape reveal.
And half disclose those Limbs it should conceal;   *10*
Of those loose Curls, that ivory front, I write;
Of the dear Web whole Volumes I indite:
Or if to Musick she the Lyre awake,
That the soft Subject of my Song I make,
And sing with what a careless Grace she flings   *15*
Her artful hand across the sounding Strings.
If sinking into Sleep she seem to close
Her languid Lids, I favour her repose.
With lulling Notes, and thousand beauties see
That Slumber brings to aid my Poetry.   *20*
When, less averse, and yielding to Desires,
She half accepts, and half rejects, my Fires;
While to retain the envious Lawn she tries,
And struggles to elude my longing Eyes,
The fruitful Muse from that auspicious Night   *25*
Dates the long Iliad of the amorous Fight.
In brief whatever she do, or say, or look,
'Tis ample Matter for a Lover's Book;
And many a copious Narrative you'll see
Big with important Nothing's History.   *30*

Yet would the tyrant Love permit me raise
My feeble voice to sound the victor's praise,
To paint the hero's toil, the ranks of war,
The laurell'd triumph and the sculptured car;
No giant race, no tumult of the skies,   35
No mountain-structures in my verse should rise.
Nor tale of Thebes, nor Ilium there should be,
Nor how the Persian trod the indignant sea;
Not Marius' Cimbrian wreaths would I relate.
Nor lofty Carthage struggling with her fate.   40
Here should Augustus great in arms appear,
And thou, Mæcenas, be my second care;
Here Mutina from flames and famine free,
And there the ensanguined wave of Sicily,
And sceptered Alexandria's captive shore,   45
And sad Philippi, red with Roman Gore:
Then, while the vaulted skies loud ïos rend,
In golden chains should loaded monarchs bend,
And hoary Nile with pensive aspect seem
To mourn the glories of his sevenfold stream,   50
While prows, that late in fierce encounter met,
Move through the sacred way and vainly threat,
Thee too the Muse should consecrate to fame,
And with her garlands weave thy ever-faithful name.
    But nor Callimachus' enervate strain   55
May tell of Jove, and Phlegra's blasted plain;
Nor I with unaccustomed vigour trace
Back to its source divine the Julian race.
Sailors to tell of winds and seas delight.
The shepherd of his flocks, the soldier of the gight,   60
A milder warfare I in verse display;
Each in his proper art should waste the day:
Nor thou my gentle calling disapprove,
To die is glorious in the bed of Love.
    Happy the youth, and not unknown to fame,   65
Whose heart has never felt a second flame.
Oh, might that envied happiness be mine!

To Cynthia all my Wishes I confine;
Or if, alas! it be my fate to try
Another love, the quicker let me die: *70*
But she, the mistress of my faithful breast,
Has oft the charms of constancy confest.
Condemns her fickle sex's fond mistake,
And hates the tale of Troy for Helen's sake.
Me from myself the soft enchantress stole;   *75*
Ah! let her ever my Desires control,
Or if I fall the victim of her scorn,
From her loved door may my pale corse be born.
The power of herbs can other harms remove,
And find a cure for every ill but love.   *80*
The Melian's hurt Machaon could repair,
Heal the slow chief, and send again to war;
To Chiron Phœnix owed his long-lost sight,
And Phœbus' son recall'd Androgeon to the light.
Here Arts are vain, e'en magick here must fail,   *85*
The powerful mixture and the midnight spell;
The hand that can my captive heart release
And to this bosom give its wonted peace,
May the long thirst of Tantalus allay,
Or drive the infernal vulture from his prey.   *90*
For ills unseen what remedy is found?
Or who can probe the undiscover'd wound?
The bed avails not, nor the leech's care,
Nor changing skies can hurt nor sultry air.
'Tis hard th' elusive symptoms to explore: *95*
To day the lover walks, to-morrow is no more;
A train of mourning friends attend his pall,
And wonder at the sudden funeral.
    When then my fates that breath they gave shall claim,
When the short Marble but preserve a name,   *100*
A little verse my all that shall remain;
Thy passing courser's slacken'd speed restrain;
(Thou envied honour of thy poet's days,
Of all our youth the ambition and the praise!)

Then to my quiet urn awhile draw near,   *105*
And say, while o'er the place you drop the tear,
Love and the fair were of his life the pride;
He lived, while she was kind; and when she frown'd, he died.

April *1742. Æt. 26*

IMITATED FROM
Propertius. Lib: 3: Eleg: 5.

Pacis amor Deus est, &c:

L ove, gentle Power! to Peace was e'er a friend;
  Before the Goddess' shrine we too, love's vot'ries, bend.
Still may his Bard in softer fights engage;
Wars hand to hand with Cynthia let me wage.

Long as of youth the joyous hours remain.   *5*
Me may Castalia's sweet recess detain.
Fast by th' umbrageous vale lull'd to repose,
Where Aganippe warbles as it flows;
Or roused by sprightly sounds from out the trance,
I'd in the ring knit hands, and joyn the Muses' dance.   *10*
Give me to send the laughing bowl around.
My soul in Bacchus' pleasing fetters bound;
Let on this head unfading flowers reside,
There bloom the vernal rose's earliest pride;
And when, our flames commission'd to destroy.   *15*
Age step 'twixt love and me, and intercept the joy;
When my changed head these locks no more shall know,
And all its jetty honours turn to snow;
Then let me rightly spell of nature's ways;
To Providence, to Him my thoughts I'd raise,   *20*
Who taught this vast machine its steadfast laws,
That first, eternal, universal Cause;

Search to what regions yonder Star retires,
Who monthly waning hides her paly fires.
And whence, anew revived, with silver light   25
Relumes her crescent Orb to cheer the dreary Night:
How riseing winds the face of Ocean sweep,
Where lie th' eternal fountains of the deep,
And whence the cloudy Magazines maintain
Their wintry war or pour the autumnal rain;   30
How flames perhaps, with dire confusion hurl'd.
Shall sink this beauteous fabric of the world;
What colours paint the vivid arch of Jove;
What wondrous force the solid earth can move.
When Pindus' self approaching ruin dreads.   35
Shakes all his Pines, and bows his hundred heads;
Why does yon Orb, so exquisitely bright.
Obscure his radiance in a short-liv'd night;
Whence the seven Sisters' congregated fires.
And what Bootes' lazy waggon tires;   40
How the rude surge its sandy Bounds control;
Who measured out the year, and bad the seasons roll;
If realms beneath those fabled torments know.
Pangs without respite, fires that ever glow.
Earth's monster-brood stretch'd on their iron bed.   45
The hissing terrors round Alecto's head,
Scarce to nine acres Tityus' bulk confined,
The triple dog that scares the shadowy kind.
All angry heaven inflicts, or hell can feel.
The pendent rock, Ixion's whirling wheel,   50
Famine at feasts, and thirst amid the stream;
Or are our fears th' enthusiast's empty dream,
And all the scenes, that hurt the grave's repose.
But pictured horrour and poetic woes?

These soft, inglorious joys my hours engage;   55
Be love my youth's pursuit and science crown my Age.
You whose young bosoms feel a nobler flame
Redeem, what Crassus lost and vindicate his name.

Notes

Gray wrote his own notes to be printed with the published poems. These are included below in sequence with the indicator [AN] following the note.

ODE ON THE SPRING, p.17

[Written at Stoke Poges in the first half of 1742, and originally sent in a letter to Richard West, who, alas, had died before receiving it. First published 1748 in Dodsley's *Collection of Poems by Several hands*. In one of the manuscript copies the poem is entitled 'Noon-Tide, An Ode'.]

5 Attic warbler: nightingale

9 *Zephyr*: wind, specifically one from the west; from *Zephyros*, Greek god of the west wind.

14 ——————————— a bank [...]
O'er-canopied with luscious woodbine.
    Shakesp. Mids. Night's Dream. [II. i. 249-51] [AN]

27 "Nare per aestatem liquidam —" [To swim through cloudless summer] *Virgil. Georg. lib. 4.* [l. 59] [AN]

30 ———— sporting with quick glance
Shew to the sun their waved coats drop'd with gold.
    Milton's Paradise Lost, book 7. [ll. 405-6] [AN]

31 While insects from the threshold preach, &c.
    M. Green, *in the Grotto.*
    Dodsley's Miscellanies, Vol. V, p. 161. [AN]

ODE ON THE DEATH OF A FAVOURITE CAT, p.19

[Written in Cambridge in Feb. 1747 and sent in a letter of 1 March 1747 to Horace Walpole, author and close friend of Gray, whose cat had suffered the fate described in the poem. First published 1748 in Dodsley's *Collection of Poems by Several hands*.]

16 *Tyrian hue*: i.e. purple. The "royal" purple dye, made from shellfish in Tyre, today in Lebanon, was a luxury item in the ancient world.

31 *Eight times* — alludes to the legend of a cat having nine lives.

34 *Nereid*: sea-nymph (Greek)

35 *Tom; Susan*: (here) generic names of servants; another manuscript version has Harry for Susan.

42 *Glisters*: glitters, glistens; the proverb is an old one and occurs in English literature as far back as Chaucer. In *The Merchant of Venice* (II, vii, 65) Shakespeare uses the phrase "All that glisters is not gold".

Dryden had also used the phrase "All… that glitters is not gold" in 'The Hind and the Panther', his longest poem (1687).

ODE ON A DISTANT PROSPECT OF ETON COLLEGE, p.21

[Gray had been a pupil at Eton from 1725-1734. Written at Stoke Poges in mid-1742. First published as a folio pamphlet by Dodsley, 30 May 1747. In two manuscript copies the title of the poem is 'Ode, on a Prospect of Windsor, & the adjacent Country'.]

4   [Henry's.] King Henry the Sixth, Founder of the College. [AN]

19 "And bees their honey redolent of spring."
    Dryden's Fable on the Pythag. System. [AN]

23 margent: banks

21-30 references to school sports: swimming, hoop rolling and ball-games.

36 descry: observe, see.

79 "——Madness laughing in his ireful mood."
    Dryden's Fable of Palamon and Arcite. [ii. 582] [AN]

HYMN TO ADVERSITY, p.25

[Also known as 'Ode to Adversity' in other manuscripts. Written in Stoke Poges by mid-1742. Sent in a letter to Walpole on 8 September 1751. First published in Dodsley's Designs, 1753.]

Epigraph: Aeschylus, Agamemnon, 161-171: "Zeus it is who has led mortals to wisdom by establishing it as a fixed law that knowledge comes by suffering."

1   Daughter of Jove: According to Homer in The Iliad, Ate (Infatuation) was the daughter of Zeus. Mitford says that Ate "may be called the goddess of Adversity".

5   adamantine: i.e. made of adamant; unbreakable

35 Gorgon terrors: the Gorgon legendarily fought by Perseus had writhing snakes in place of hair and her gaze would turn men to stone.

THE PROGRESS OF POESY, p.27

[Pindaric ode: Pindar was a Greek poet of the 5th century BC. His odes were ceremonial poems performed to celebrate a victor in one of the classical Games, the Olympiad being the most famous of them today. Written at some point between 1751 and December 1754, when Gray sent it in a letter to Thomas Wharton. First published as 'Ode' in *Odes by Mr Gray*, 1757.]

1   Psalm LVII, 8 "Awake, my glory; awake, psaltery [sic] and harp." Pindar styles his own poetry with its musical accompanyments, Aeolian song, Aeolian strings, the breath of the Aeolian flute. [AN]

     Aeolian: Pindar was an Aeolian poet, i.e. one whose dialect was Aeolian, spoken in Thebes and more widely throughout Boeotia.

3   The subject and simile, as usual with Pindar, are united. The various sources of poetry, which gives life and lustre to all it touches, are here described; its quiet majestic progress enriching every subject (otherwise dry and barren) with a pomp of diction and luxuriant harmony of numbers; and its more rapid and irresistible course, when swoln and hurried away by the conflict of tumultuous passions. [AN]

     Helicon: the mountain in Boeotia, home to the Muses and to two sacred springs.

9   Ceres: Greek goddess of the harvest.

13   Power of harmony to calm the turbulent sallies of the soul. The thoughts are borrowed from the first Pythian of Pindar. [See note to l. 20.] [AN]

17   Thracia: an area that today consists roughly of southern Bulgaria, north-eastern Greece, and European Turkey. In ancient times it came under both Persian and Hellenistic control at various times, before falling under Roman control.

17   Lord of War: Ares (or Mars). Ares was the most important of the Greek gods in Thrace.

18   car: chariot

20   This is a weak imitation of some incomparable lines in the same Ode. [Pindar, *Pythian Ode* I, 1-12.] [AN]

25   Power of harmony to produce all the graces of motion in the body. [AN]

27   Idalia: Idalion, a town in Cyprus where there was a famous temple to the goddess Aphrodite. The modern village of Dali, in the district of Nicosia, is near the site.

29   Cytherea: Cythera is an island S.E. of the Peleponnese peninsula, and has a famous temple to Aphrodite.

35   "He (Odysseus) gazed at the quick twinkling of (the dancers') feet; and he wondered in his heart." Homer. *Od[yssey]*. O. [viii. 265]. [AN]

41   "And on his rose-red cheeks there gleams the light of love." Phrynichus, apud Athenaeum. [*Deipnosophistae*, xiii. 604a] [AN]

42 To compensate the real and imaginary ills of life, the Muse was given to Mankind by the same Providence that sends the Day by its chearful presence to dispel the gloom and terrors of the Night. [AN]

52 Or seen the Morning's well-appointed Star
    Come marching up the eastern hills afar.
        Cowley. [Brutus, an Ode, st. 4] [AN]

53 Hyperion: one of the Titans, and father of the sun, moon and stars. His name is often used to stand for the sun, and thus Hyperion's march is the progress of the sun across the sky.

54 Extensive influence of poetic Genius over the remotest and most uncivilized nations: its connection with liberty, and the virtues that naturally attend on it. [See the Erse, Norwegian, and Welch Fragments, the Lapland and American songs.] [AN]

    solar road: "Extra anni solisque vias—" [Beyond the paths of the year and the sun—] Virgil. [*Aeneid*, vi. 796] [AN]

    "Tutta lontana dal camin del sole." [Quite far from the road of the sun.] Petrarch, Canzon 2. [*Canzoniere*, 'Canzone II', l. 48] [AN]

66 Progress of Poetry from Greece to Italy, and from Italy to England. Chaucer was not unacquainted with the writings of Dante or of Petrarch. The Earl of Surrey and Sir Tho. Wyatt had travelled in Italy, and formed their taste there; Spenser imitated the Italian writers; Milton improved on them: but this School expired soon after the Restoration, and a new one arose on the French model, which has subsisted ever since. [AN]

68 Ilissus: Ilisos, a river that, in antiquity, ran outside the defensive walls of Athens. Today it is now mostly underground.

69 Maeander: a river (Maiandros) in southern Anatolia, now Turkey. The English word "meander" derives from the river's name, which was well-known for its winding course. In ancient times, it reached the Aegean near the city of Miletus. Maeander was also the name of the river-god associated with this area.

77 the Nine: the Muses.

78 Parnassus: home of the Muses; Mount Helicon.

78 Latian plains: the lands around Rome.

81 Latium: see also n. line 78. Region of west central Italy which was the home of the Latin tribes, and where Rome is situated. Today part of the (larger) Italian province of Lazio. *Here* Latium stands for Rome.

82 Albion: Britain.

84 Nature's Darling: Shakespear. [AN]

95   He: Milton. [AN]

96   seraph: angel.

98   "—flammantia moenia mundi." [—the flaming ramparts of the world]. Lucretius. [*De Rerum Natura*, i. 74] [AN]

99   For the spirit of the living creature was in the wheels—And above the firmament, that was over their heads, was the likeness of a throne, as the appearance of a saphire-stone.—This was the appearance [of the likeness] of the glory of the Lord. *Ezekiel* i. 20, 26, 28. [AN]

102 (the Muse) took away (his) eyes, but she gave (him the gift of) sweet song]. Homer. Od[yssey, viii. 64]. [AN]

103 car: chariot. Dryden (1631-1700): poet laureate and perhaps the greatest English poet of the second half of the 17th century. Apart from his own works, he made a magnificent translation of Virgil's *Aeneid*.

105 Meant to express the stately march and sounding energy of Dryden's rhimes. [AN]

106 Hast thou cloathed his neck with thunder? *Job*. [xxxix. 19] [AN]

110 Words, that weep, and tears, that speak. Cowley. ["The Prophet" in *The Mistress*, line 20] [AN]

111 We have had in our language no other odes of the sublime kind, than that of Dryden on St. Cecilia's day: for Cowley (who had his merit) yet wanted judgment, style, and harmony, for such a task. That of Pope is not worthy of so great a man. Mr. Mason indeed of late days has touched the true chords, and with a masterly hand, in some of his Choruses,—above all in the last of Caractacus,

   Hark! heard ye not yon footstep dread? &c. [AN]

115 "against the god-like bird of Zeus" [Pindar] *Olymp*. 2. [88] Pindar compares himself to that bird, and his enemies to ravens that croak and clamour in vain below, while it pursues its flight, regardless of their noise. [AN]

THE BARD, p.32

[Written 1754-57. First published 1757 in *Odes by Mr Gray*.]

4   Mocking the air with colours idly spread. Shakespear's *King John*. [V. i. 72] [AN]

5   The Hauberk was a texture of steel ringlets, or rings interwoven, forming a coat of mail, that sate close to the body, and adapted itself to every motion. [AN]

8 Cambria: Wales

9 — [By] The crested adder's pride. Dryden's *Indian Queen*. [III. i. 84] [AN]

11 *Snowdon* was a name given by the Saxons to that mountainous tract, which the Welch themselves call *Craigian-eryri*: it included all the highlands of Caernarvonshire and Merionethshire, as far east as the river Conway. R. Hygden[,] speaking of the castle of Conway built by King Edward the first, says, "Ad ortum amnis Conway ad clivum montis Erery [At the source of the River Conway on the slope of Mt. Erery];" and Matthew of Westminster, (ad ann. 1283,) "Apud Aberconway ad pedes montis Snowdoniae fecit erigi castrum forte [Near (or at) Aberconway at the foot of Mt. Snowdon, he caused a fortified camp to be constructed.]." [AN]

13 Gilbert de Clare, surnamed the Red, Earl of Gloucester and Hertford, son-in-law to King Edward. [AN]

Stout Gloucester: Gilbert de Clare (1243-1295), driven out of Wales by an uprising in 1294. Spent many years fighting in Wales.

14 Edmond de Mortimer, Lord of Wigmore. They both were *Lords-Marchers*, whose lands lay on the borders of Wales, and probably accompanied the King in this expedition. [AN]

18 ["...*haggard*, wch conveys to you the Idea of a *Witch*, is indeed only a metaphor taken from an unreclaim'd Hawk, wch is called a *Haggard*, & looks wild & *farouche* & jealous of its liberty." Letter to Wharton, 21 Aug. 1755.] [AN]

19 The image was taken from a well-known picture of Raphael, representing the Supreme Being in the vision of Ezekiel: there are two of these paintings (both believed original), one at Florence, the other at Paris. [AN]

20 Shone, like a meteor, streaming to the wind. Milton's *Paradise Lost*. [i. 537] [AN]

28, 29, 31 Hoel, Llewellyn, Cadwallo, Urien: Welsh bards

33 Modred: Also Mordred, the villain of the Arthurian legends. *Possibly* meant to be Myrddin (Merlin), the legendary magician.

34 Plinlimmon: a mountain on the border of Powys and Ceredigion. Source of the rivers Wye and Severn.

35 The shores of Caernarvonshire opposite to the isle of Anglesey. [AN]

38 Cambden and others observe, that eagles used annually to build their aerie among the rocks of Snowdon, which from thence (as some think) were named by the Welch *Craigian-eryri*, or the crags of the eagles. At this day (I am told) the highest point of Snowdon is called the *eagle's*

nest. That bird is certainly no stranger to this island, as the Scots, and the people of Cumberland, Westmoreland, &c. can testify: it even has built its nest in the Peak of Derbyshire. [See Willoughby's *Ornithol.* published by Ray.] [AN]

40   As dear to me as are the ruddy drops,
       That visit my sad heart—
           Shakesp. *Jul. Caesar.* [II. i. 289-90] [AN]

47   See the Norwegian Ode, that follows. [i.e. The Fatal Sisters, *ed.*] [AN]

54   Edward the Second, cruelly butchered in Berkley-Castle [in 1327 near the Severn River in western England]. [AN]

57   Isabel of France, Edward the Second's adulterous Queen. [AN]

58   tear'st the bowels: refers to the grotesque fate of Edward II.

59   Triumphs of Edward the Third in France. [AN]

64   Death of that King, abandoned by his Children, and even robbed in his last moments by his Courtiers and his Mistress. [AN]

67   Edward, the Black Prince, dead some time before his Father. [AN]

71   Magnificence of Richard the Second's reign. See Froissard, and other contemporary Writers. [AN]

77   Richard the Second, (as we are told by Archbishop Scroop and the confederate Lords in their manifesto, by Thomas of Walsingham, and all the older Writers,) was starved to death [in 1400]. The story of his assassination by Sir Piers of Exon, is of much later date. [AN]

83   Ruinous civil wars of York and Lancaster. [AN]

87   Henry the Sixth, George Duke of Clarence, Edward the Fifth, Richard Duke of York, &c. believed to be murthered secretly in the Tower of London. The oldest part of that structure is vulgarly attributed to Julius Caesar. [AN]

89   Consort: Margaret of Anjou, a woman of heroic spirit, who struggled hard to save her Husband and her Crown. [AN]

       Father: Henry the Fifth. [AN]

90   Henry the Sixth very near being canonized. The line of Lancaster had no right of inheritance to the Crown. [AN]

91   The white and red roses, devices of York and Lancaster [presumably woven above and below on the loom]. [AN]

92   The silver Boar was the badge of Richard the Third; whence he was usually known in his own time by the name of *the Boar.* [AN]

99   Eleanor of Castile died a few years after the conquest of Wales. The heroic proof she gave of her affection for her Lord [she is supposed

to have sucked the poison from a wound Edward I received] is well known. The monuments of his regret, and sorrow for the loss of her, are still to be seen at Northampton, Geddington, Waltham, and other places. [AN]

109 It was the common belief of the Welch nation, that King Arthur was still alive in Fairy-Land, and should return again to reign over Britain. [AN]

110 Both Merlin [Myrddin] and Taliessin had prophesied, that the Welch should regain their sovereignty over this island; which seemed to be accomplished in the House of Tudor [1768]. [AN]

Accession of the House of Tudor [1757]. [AN]

117 Speed relating an audience given by Queen Elizabeth to Paul Dzialinski, Ambassadour of Poland, says, 'And thus she, lion-like rising, daunted the malapert Orator no less with her stately port and majestical deporture, than with the tartnesse of her princelie checkes.' [John Speed (1552-1629) published his *History of Great Britaine... to ... King James* in 1611.] [AN]

121 Taliessin, Chief of the Bards, flourished in the VIth Century. His works are still preserved, and his memory held in high veneration among his Countrymen. [His Book exists in only a thirteenth-century version and many of the poems in it may not be by Taliessin.] [AN]

126 Fierce wars and faithful loves shall moralize my song.
    Spenser's Proëme to the *Fairy Queen* [l. 9]. [AN]

128 Shakespear [AN]

131 Milton [AN]

133 The succession of Poets after Milton's time. [AN]

The Fatal Sisters, p.38

[Written 1761. First published 1768 in *Poems by Mr Gray*.]

Note — The *Valkyriur* were female Divinities, Servants of *Odin* (or *Woden*) in the Gothic mythology. Their name signifies *Chusers of the slain*. They were mounted on swift horses, with drawn swords in their hands; and in the throng of battle selected such as were destined to slaughter, and conducted them to *Valhalla*, the hall of *Odin*, or paradise of the Brave; where they attended the banquet, and served the departed Heroes with horns of mead and ale. [AN]

3   How quick they wheel'd; and flying, behind them shot
    Sharp sleet of arrowy shower—
        Milton's *Paradise Regained*. [iii. 323-4] [AN]

4   The noise of battle hurtled in the air.
    Shakespear's *Jul. Caesar.* [II. ii. 22] [AN]

6   dusky warp: refers to the Fates (in Norse myth, four sisters) weaving
    the events of the world.

8   woe: here refers to Earl Sigurd; bane = slayer of Randver, referring
    here to Odin father of the Gods. Randver may be the 8th century
    Swedish king of that name.

17-18 Mista, Sangrida, Hilda: valkyries.

31 Gondula and Geira: valkyries.

45 Eirin: Ireland.

62 faulchion: a short sword used in medieval times. From Ital. *falcione*
    and, in turn, Latin *falx*, sickle).

THE DESCENT OF ODIN, p.43

[Written 1761. First published 1768 in *Poems by Mr Gray.*]

4   *Niflheimr*, the hell of the Gothic nations, consisted of nine worlds,
    to which were devoted all such as died of sickness, old-age, or by any
    other means than in battle: Over it presided *Hela*, the Goddess of
    Death. [AN]

5   Dog of darkness: Garm, the dog who guarded the gates of hell.

16 nine of hell: the nine realms of the Norse mythology, although Gray
    mistakenly assumes them all to be of the underworld.

37 Traveller: Odin travels in disguise, under the name *Vegtamr*, or
    Wanderer.

46 Balder: god of light in Norse mythology; son of Odin and Frigg. His
    death was to herald the end of days, or *Ragnarök*.

55 Hoder: (also Hod, Hodur, Höðr, was the unwitting cause of Balder's
    death. Baldr's mother, Frigg, had insisted that everyone and everything
    should swear never to harm Balder, except for the mistletoe, which
    she regarded as too unimportant to ask. The gods gained much
    amusement by trying out weapons on Baldr, to no effect. Loki, the
    trickster, when he disocvered Balder's sole weakness, made a missile
    from mistletoe, and helped Hoder fire it at Balder. Odin and the
    giantess Rinda then gave birth to Váli, who grew to adulthood within
    a day and slew Hoder.

65 Rinda: see 55 above

90 *Lok* is the evil Being, who continues in chains till the *Twilight of
    the Gods* approaches, when he shall break his bonds; the human
    race, the stars, and sun, shall disappear; the earth sink in the seas,

and fire consume the skies: even *Odin* himself and his kindred-deities shall perish. For a farther explanation of this mythology, see Mallet's Introduction to the *History of Denmark*, 1755, Quarto. [AN]

THE TRIUMPHS OF OWEN, p.47

[Written 1760/61. First published 1768 in *Poems by Mr Gray*.]

3   Roderic: Roderic the Great (Rhodri Mawr) ruler of Wales in the 10th century. Owain Gwynedd (Owen Gwyneth) was his direct descendant.

4   Gwyneth, Gwynned or Gwynedd: North-Wales. [AN]

11   Eirin: Ireland

14   Lochlin: Denmark. [AN]

20   The Dragon-son: The red Dragon is the device of Cadwallader, which all his descendents bore on their banners. [AN]

25   Talymalfra: Moelfre, a bay on the NE coast of Anglesey.

ELEGY, p.50

[Written 1745-50. Published 1751 as a stand-alone pamphlet. Reprinted in *Designs by Mr R Bentley...* in 1753 (2 editions), again in 1762, coupled with 'Hymn to Adversity', in a miscellany in 6 volumes, by various hands in 1765, in 1768 in *Poems by Mr Gray* (London, Glasgow, Dublin and Cork editions, and in the 1771 editions (London & Dublin) of *Poems by Mr Gray. A New Edition.*]

1   tolls:

        [Era gia l' ora, che volge 'l disio
        A' naviganti, e 'ntenerisce 'l cuore
        Lo di ch' han detto a' dolci amici addio:
        E che lo nuovo peregrin d' amore
        Punge, se ode] — squilla di lontano
        Che paia 'l giorno pianger, che si muore.
        [(It was already the hour which turns back the desire
        Of the sailors, and melts their hearts,
        The day that they have said good-bye to their sweet friends,
        And which pierces the new pilgrim with love,
        If he hears) — from afar the bell
        Which seems to mourn the dying day.]
                Dante. *Purgat.* l. 8. [Canto 8 lines i-vi.] [AN]

57   village-Hampden: refers to John Hampden, a leading Parliamentarian, whose attempted unconstitutional arrest by King Charles I in the House of Commons (1642) marks the beginning of the Civil War.

59-60 Milton, Cromwell: Milton was the greatest literary figure of the Parliamentarian side in the Civil War; Oliver Cromwell was the political and military leader.

92   Ch'i veggio nel pensier, dolce mio fuoco,
Fredda una lingua, & due begli occhi chiusi
Rimaner doppo noi pien di faville.
[For I see in my thoughts, my sweet fire,
One cold tongue, and two beautiful closed eyes
Will remain full of sparks after our death.]
Petrarch. *Son.* 169. [AN]

127 — paventosa speme. [— fearful hope]
Petrarch. *Son.* 114. [AN]

A LONG STORY, p.57

"[Lady Cobham, then living at Stoke Poges, after reading the Elegy was anxious to make Gray's acquaintance. Miss Speed and Lady Schaub, who were staying with her, brought this about by calling on the poet. They found him out, but Gray returned the call and so the acquaintance began. Gray wrote an account of this first visit, which he called 'A Long Story'. The MS. at Pembroke is dated August 1750; the poem cannot have been finished before October, because of the allusion to Macleane in line 120. It was only once published with Gray's authority in his lifetime, in the Six Poems with Bentley's Designs in 1753, from which the present text is taken and from which Bentley's sketch drawing of Stoke Manor, after a rough sketch by Gray, is reproduced [on the next page]. It was also printed in the Dublin edition of 1768.]"

(from *The Poems of Gray and Collins.* Edited by Austin Lane Poole. Revised by Leonard Whibley. Third edition. Oxford editions of standard authors series. London: Oxford UP, 1937, reprinted 1950 [1st ed. 1919], 102.)

3   Huntingdons and Hattons: Henry Hastings, Earl of Huntingdon, rebuilt the manor-house in the reign of Elizabeth I; the house came down to Lady Coke, widow of Lord Chief Justice Coke, who was granted the manor in 1621 by King James I. Lady Coke herself was descended from the Hatton family.

11   Hatton [Lord Chancellor], prefer'd by Queen Elizabeth for his graceful Person and fine Dancing. [AN]

25   cap-a-pee: literally, head-to-foot, but presumably indicates that she is dressed in the height of current French fashion.

31   Cobham: Lady Cobham. See introductory note above.

37   capucine: hood.

103 Styack: The House-Keeper. [AN]

115 Squib: Groom of the Chambers. [AN]

116 Groom: The Steward. [AN]

120 Macleane: A famous Highwayman hang'd the week before. [AN]

144 Rubbers: games of cards, perhaps whist.

ODE FOR MUSIC, p.62

[Written 1769; published on its own the same year as *Ode performed in the Senate-house at Cambridge, 1769*. Collected in *Poems by Thomas Gray*, 1771.]

2   Comus: character in the eponymous poem by Milton; the name signifies "revels". He was the son of Circe and Bacchus, according to Milton. Thus "Comus and his midnight-crew" suggests a group devoted to excessive drinking and partying.

25   Newton: Sir Isaac Newton (1642-1727), the great mathematician and physicist, like Milton, was a Cambridge scholar, and their lives overlapped. Besides his intellectual fame, Newton was renowned for his humility.

29   Camus: the River Cam, which flows through Cambridge.

32   Cynthia: Cynthia is a generic name for a woman who is the object of desire, but is also the addressee of the love poems of Sextus Propertius, whom Gray translated. See note on p.145 below.

39   Edward: Edward III (1312-1377), who claimed the French throne in 1340, added the French *fleurs de lys* to his coat of arms.

40   Gallia: Gaul, i.e. France.

41   Chatillon: Mary de Valentia, daughter of Guy de Chatillon, and Countess of Pembroke, founded Pembroke College, Cambridge. Tradition had it that her husband, Audemars de Valentia, Earl of Pembroke, was killed in a tournament on the day of their marriage. In fact he died three years after their marriage, while in France on a diplomatic mission.

42   Clare: Elizabeth de Burg, Countess of Clare, who re-founded University Hall, Cambridge, as Clare Hall. She was married to a grandson of Edward I.

43   Anjou's Heroine: Margaret of Anjou (1430?-1482), wife of Henry VI, who founded Queen's College, Cambridge in 1448; paler rose: Elizabeth Woodville, wife of Edward IV, a scion of the House of York, whose sigil was the white rose.

45   either Henry: Henry VI and Henry VIII, the first-named being the founder of King's College and the latter a benefactor of Trinity College; majestic Lord: Henry VIII.

46   the murther'd Saint: Henry VI.

51   Granta: another name for the River Cam.

54   Fitzroy: Duke of Grafton, whose family name came from an illegitimate son of the King, Fitzroy being an anglicisation of *fils du roi*, son of the King.

66   Marg'ret; Lady Margaret Beaufort, Countess of Richmond and Derby, and mother of Henry VII. She founded Christ's College in 1505 and St John's in 1508.

70   Beaufort: Lady Margaret (see 66 above) was a Beaufort and married a Tudor.

86   fasces: a bundle of rods wrapped around an axe, carried by the lictors who walked before Roman consuls. A symbol of consular authority and temporal power.

93   Star of Brunswick: Brunswick (Braunschweig) was the ruling house in Gray's day. The Duke of Brunswick-Lüneburg was the Elector of Hanover and thus he is the "guiding star" of George III of the Hanoverian dynasty and of England.

On Lord Holland's Seat Near Margate, Kent, p.66

[Written 1768; published in the *Gentleman's Magazine* 1769, but not collected until the 1798 edition of the *The Poetical Works of Thomas Gray*.

Gosse, in his 1874 edition of Gray's works, says, "In June 1766, after Gray had been spending two months with 'Reverend Billy', the Rev. William Robinson, at his rectory of Denton, in Kent, these verses were found in a drawer of the room he had occupied. The first four stanzas (lines 1-16) were printed in the supplement to the *Gentleman's Magazine* for 1777. The two last stanzas (lines 17-24) were added incorrectly in the same periodical for February 1778, and the text finally corrected in February 1782. The house was that built for Lord Holland in imitation of Cicero's Formian villa at Baiae, by Lord Newborough."

Lord Holland, the 1st Baron Holland, was Henry Fox (1705-1774) son of Sir Stephen Fox who had accompanied Charles II to Holland.]

6   Godwin ... sand: The Goodwin Sands is a sandbank, some 10 kms in length, at the entrance to the Straits of Dover, and is a hazard to shipping. Tradition had it that the sandbank was the remains of sunken island, Lomea, which had belonged to the Saxon Earl Godwin of Wessex, father of King Harold, in the early 11th century. The tradition is fanciful.

17   Bute: Lord Bute, Prime Minister, 1762-3. Gray had hoped for preferment to the professorship of Modern History at Cambridge,

but, although he managed to have his name suggested to Bute, his campaign failed. Holland was associated with Bute for a while.

18 Shelburn, Rigby, Calcraft: Lord Holland in a satiric poem 'Lord Holland returning from Italy' had attacked these three men, who had previously been political allies.

23 Quire: choir (in the architectural sense: the part of the cathedral where the choir-singers perform).

24 foxes: a reference to Holland's family name.

AGRIPPINA, p.79

['Agrippina' was begun in London in December, 1741. The first scene was sent to West in Hertfordshire about 31st March, 1742. Gray abandoned it, having apparently decided not to pursue a long poem.]

5 Lictor: a cross between a civil servant and a bodyguard, attendant upon a magistrate in the Roman Republic.

6 Germanicus: Germanicus Julius Caesar (15BC–19AD), husband of Agrippina, and father of Nero, Drusus and Caligula, among others. He gained the additional name, Germanicus, after conquering the German tribes in revenge for the catastrophic Roman defeat in the Teutoburg Forest—where the legions had lost their eagles (regimental insignia), an event regarded as national dishonour. Agrippina herself was a granddaughter of Emperor Augustus.

7 Antium: modern Anzio, a port in the province of Latium, some 30 miles south of Rome. Birthplace of Nero.

14 Britannicus: Tiberius Claudius Caesar Britannicus (41-55 AD), son of Emperor Claudius and Messalina. His father, who had conquered Britain, was granted this honorific name, but declined it in favour of his son.

50 Julian: refers to Julius Caesar.

99 Rubellius: Rubellius Plautus (33-62 AD), a Roman noble and rival to Emperor Nero, he was a member of the greater Julian family, being descended from Octavia Minor, sister of Augustus. He was ordered executed by Nero for plotting against the throne.

100 Sylla: Lucius Cornelius Sylla (more commonly *Sulla*, ca.138-78 BC), subject of a play by Plutarch, which Dryden had translated. He was an enormously successful general, was elected Consul on two occasions and also revived the office of Dictator in order to push through reforms during a period of strife. Unlike most subsequent Dictators, he resigned his office voluntarily and went into retirement.

108 Germania: the German lands within the Roman Empire.

109 Parthian: the Parthians were a people in Asia Minor (modern Anatolia) who had been subject to the Persian Empire, but had also taken it over at one point.

110 Corbulo: Gnaeus Domitius Corbulo (*ca.* 7–67 AD), Roman general, brother-in-law of Emperor Caligula and father-in-law of Domitian.

115 Praetorian: the Praetorian Guard was the Emperor's personal guard-force.

117 Juno: Queen of the Gods in the Roman pantheon.

122 Soranus: Quintus Marcius Barea Soranus — Roman Senator during the reign of Nero, who fell afoul of the Emperor for not being hard enough on his subjects. He was accused of intriguing against the Emperor with Gaius Rubellius Plautus (see n. line 99 above), and was condemned to death in 65/66 AD. He committed suicide.

123 Cassius, Vetus, Thasea:

Gaius Cassius Longinus, direct descendant of the man who plotted against Julius Caesar. Legal theorist who held several administrative posts in Rome and in Asia Minor. Exiled by Nero to Sardinia in 65 AD, but returned when Vespasian became Emperor.

Lucius Antistius Vetus: Consul with Nero in 55 AD; Senator, and later Pro-Consul in Asia. Accused of plotting against Nero, he committed suicide with his daughter, 66 AD.

Publius Clodius Thrasea Paetus (d. 66 AD): Senator and opponent of Nero, found guilty of treason by the Senate and ordered to commit suicide.

148 Burrhus: Praefect of the Praetorian Guard when Nero came to the throne.

171 Syllani: (or, *Sullani*), i.e. followers of Sylla/Sulla (see 100 above).

183 Otho, Poppaea: Marcus Salvius Otho Caesar Augustus (32 –69 AD), Emperor for three months, from 15 January to 16 April 69; Poppaea was his wife, with whom Nero fell in love and whom he later married.

SONNET ON THE DEATH OF MR RICHARD WEST, p.87

[Written 1742. Published 1775 in *The Poems of Mr. Gray. To which are prefixed Memoirs of his Life and Writings by W[illiam]. Mason.* and *Poems by Mr. Gray. A new edition* (editions in London, 1776, and Edinburgh & Dublin, 1775. Richard West was Gray's closest friend at Eton, and was the son of Richard West, Lord-Chancellor of Ireland, who died at the age of 35.]

2 Phoebus: Apollo. Gray refers here to the sun, which Apollo was supposed
to have pulled across the sky.

HYMN TO IGNORANCE, p.87

[Written in the winter of 1742, in Cambridge, but left unfinished.]

3   Camus: the River Cam in Cambridge.

11 Hyperion: in Greek mythology, one of the Titan offspring of Gaia (the
    earth-goddess) and Uranus (the sky-god) who overthrew Uranus only
    to be overthrown themselves by the Olympian gods. Hyperion was the
    father of Helios (Sun), Selene (moon) and Eos (Dawn).

14 Ægis: a protective device, perhaps a kind of supernatural shield, or
    cover, which was carried by Athena and Zeus, according to the *Iliad*.
    There is a possible etymological connection with Aex / Aix, one of the
    daughters of Helios and a mistress of Zeus.

17 Lethean: the River Lethe was one of the five rivers of Hades. All who
    drank from it experienced complete amnesia.

24: ebon: i.e. ebony, black.

36 Grandam: old woman, grandmother.

27 Sesostris: an Egyptian king, who, according to Herodotus, led a
    military force into Europe. There is no record of such an expedition
    however, nor of a Pharaoh by that name. It is thought possible that
    the name used by Herodotus is a corruption of Senusret (a ruler of
    the 12th dynasty), who did invade the area now known as Lebanon.
    Given the extensive trade relations between the Hellenic world and the
    Levantine coastline, stories of any such invasion would have reached
    the Greeks quickly.

THE ALLIANCE OF EDUCATION AND GOVERNMENT, p.89

[Written 1748-9. The first 57 lines were sent in a letter to Dr Wharton in
August 1748. Published in 1775.]

47 Scythia: a part of western Asia bordering the Black Sea and Caspian
    Sea. The Scythians were defeated by Philip of Macedon, father of
    Alexander the Great.

51 Myriads: in ancient Greek, a myriad is the number 10,000, although
    this has metamorphosed in modern times to mean simply a very large
    number.

77 Zembla: possible reference to Novaya Zemlya (*Russian*, lit. 'new land')
    an ice-bound island in the Arctic.

STANZAS TO MR BENTLEY. p.93

[Written 1752, in thanks to Bentley for providing the drawings in the collection *Six Poems*, 1753. Richard Bentley was the son of the Master of Trinity College, and was an adviser to Horace Walpole in the creation and decoration of the latter's mock-Gothic Strawberry Hill house in Twickenham. He also assisted with the publications of Walpole's Strawberry Hill press.]

15 Pope: Alexander Pope (1688-1744), also a Twickenham resident, and the leading poet of his day.

16 Dryden: John Dryden (1631-1700), poet laureate and the leading poet of the second half of the 17th century.

SATIRE ON THE HEADS OF HOUSES, p.103

[Written after 1747, but not published until 1884. The Houses are Cambridge colleges; names that are listed here differently from their modern versions are: Maudlin (Magdalene); Sidney (Sidney Sussex); Keys (Caius) Benet — or Bene't (Corpus Christi).]

[TOPHET], p.104

[Satire on the Rev. Henry Etough, a Jewish convert to Christianity, he was supposed to have gained extensive knowledge of the private affairs and history of all the great families, which led to his being regarded with some suspicion. First published 1783.]

1 Tophet: supposedly, a location in Jerusalem where pagans sacrificed children to the gods. This legend owes his its origins to a rabbinic commentary. By analogy, Tophet became, in Christian theology, a synonym for hell. According to Bradshaw (1891), Tophet is however a misprint for Etough which occurred at the first printing. Tophet could however be simply an anagrammic pun on Etough (if pronounced *Etoff*, rather than *Ettow*).

INVITATION TO MASON, p.105

[Written 1767/8, and sent in a letter to Mason dated 8 January. 1768.]

1 Prim Hurd: according to Mitford's note on the manuscript, this is a Mr Weddell, of Newby, who made a collection of statues, later sold to Lord de Grey, while on tour with Palgrave in Italy. Palgrave was a fellow of Pembroke College.

2 Delaval was also a Fellow of Pembroke and a Fellow of the Royal Society.

3   Powell: William Samuel Powell, elected Master of St John's College, 1764; Marriott: Sir James Marriot, Master of Trinity Hall 1764-1803.

4   Glyn: Glyn was Gray's doctor in Cambridge, and a close friend; Tom Nevile: Thomas Neville, Fellow of Jesus College and translator of Horace, Juvenal and Virgil.

5   Brown: Dr James Brown, Fellow and, from 1770, Master of Pembroke. With Mason he was joint executor of Gray's will.

8   Balguy: Dr Thomas Balguy of St John's, who declined a bishopric.

COUPLET ABOUT BIRDS, p.105

[Written 1763-67. According to Gray's friend, Mr Nicholls, this was extemporised while on a morning walk.]

PARODY ON AN EPITAPH, p.105

[Written 1767. According to Bradshaw in the 1891 edition of Gray's works, the epitaph being parodied was:

"Who Faith, Love, Mercy, noble Constancy
To God, to Virtue, to Distress, to Right
Observed, expressed, showed, held religiously
Hath here this monument thou seest in sight,
The cover of her earthly part, but passenger
Know Heaven and Fame contains the best of her."

"It is on an altar tomb, with recumbent figure, in the chancel of Appleby Church; the monument was erected in 1617, to Margaret (Russell), widow of George Clifford, 3rd Earl of Cumberland, by her only daughter, Anne, successively Countess of Dorset and of Pembroke and Montgomery; her own tomb, for which she also wrote the inscription, stands opposite."

3   The four names are those of castles inherited by the Countess.

IMPROMPTUS, p.106

— on Dr K[eene]

[Written after 1753. Edmund Keene (1714-1781) Bishop of Chester, and then Ely, was not a great favourite of Gray's.]

— on Raby Castle

[Raby, Co. Durham, was the seat of Henry Vane (1705-1758), Lord Barnard, first Earl of Darlington.

LINES ON DR ROBERT SMITH, p.107

[Written after 1742. First published in the Gosse edition of Gray's works (1906) and according to the editor, "written on the occasion of the threatened destruction of the Chestnuts at Trinity by Dr. Robert Smith (1689-1768), Master of that college, and author of a treatise on Optics, in consequence of which he got the nickname of Old Focus. They [the lines] were preserved by Prof. Adam Sedgwick."

LINES SPOKEN BY THE GHOST..., p.108

[Written 1734. The earliest extant poem by Gray. It was sent to Walpole on 8 December, 1734. First published in 1915. John Dennis (1657-1734) was an early 18th-century literary critic, frequent opponent of Pope, and perennially short of money.]

DANTE'S INFERNO xxxiii 1-78, p.115

[Possibly written around 1738, when Gray was translating Tasso.]

STATIUS: THEBAID VI, 646-88; 704-24, p.118

[Translation made *ca.* 1736, and sent in a letter to West. Statius was Publius Papinius Statius (*ca.* 45-96 AD); his *Thebaid* is an epic poem in twelve books on the seven champions of Argos and their unsuccessful battle against the city of Thebes. Their mission was to rest the throne of Thebes from Eteocles (son of Oedipus), who had usurped it from his own brother, Polynices. The same story had been covered in the early Greek epic *Thebais*, which today only survives in fragments and whose author is unknown. A later treatment of the theme by Antimachus of Colophon, also titled *Thebais*, may have had some influence on Statius. A more local influence was, however, Virgil's *Aeneid*, the most substantial and the best-known of all Latin epics.]

STATIUS: THEBAID IX, 646-88; 319-26, p.121

[Date of composition unknown, but Walpole is on record as having said they were written while the poet was still at Eton.]

TASSO: GERUSALEMME LIBERATA, 14, St. 32, p.122

[Translation made before September 1738. Torquato Tasso (1544-1595) was one of the most influential Italian Renaissance poets; his *Gerusalemme Liberata* (Jerusalem Liberated) concerns the capture of Jerusalem by Godfrey of Bouillon (Godefroi de Bouillon) in the First Crusade. The poem's hero, a fictional figure, is Rinaldo d'Este.]

3   Ascalon: modern Ashkelon, in Israel. A significant battle took place there in 1099, after the seizure of Jerusalem. Godfrey's army defeated the Muslim army, a multi-racial force led by an Arab vizier from the Fatimid court in Egypt.

17   Boreas: the north wind.

55   Po, Danubius: the Po and Danube rivers.

IMITATED FROM PROPERTIUS: Lib:2, Eleg:1, p.124

[Composed before 23 April 1742, when Gray sent it in a latter to West. Sextus Propertius (*ca.* 50-15 BC) was a friend of both Virgil and Ovid, and wrote a number of love elegies to his mistress Hostia, who goes by the name Cynthia in the poems. Maecenas is Gaius Cilnius Maecenas (*ca.* 70-8 BC) was a Roman statesman and famous patron, whose name has become proverbial for his munificence and support for an artist.]

5   Phoebus: Apollo

37   Thebes ... Ilium: Thebes is a Greek city in Boeotia (modern Thiva), with a past stretching back into the days of legend (Cadmus, Oedipus and Dionysus). It was destroyed by Macedonian forces under Philip II and Alexander. Ilium is Troy.

38   Persian: Thebes threw in its lot with the invading Persians, as they were perennial rivals of Athens.

38   Marius' Cimbrian: The Cimbrian war (113–102 BC) was a struggle between Rome and the Germanic tribes of the Cimbri (from modern Jutland and southern Scandinavia) and the Teutones, who had migrated into Roman territory and threatened the Roman heartlands in Italy. The general who won the war was Gaius Marius, uncle to Julius Caesar; he was a significant reformer and political force as consul as well as being a military man.

40   Carthage: initially a Phoenician colony in what is now Tunisia, and Rome's great rival in the Mediterranean until the Carthaginian forces were destroyed in the Third Punic War, and the city razed in 146 BC. It was refounded as a Roman city, only to be finally destroyed once again during the Muslim conquest in 698.

43   Mutina: Battle of Mutina (21 April, 43 BC) fought between the armies of Mark Antony and Aulus Hirtius and Octavian, one year after the assassination of Julius Caesar. This battle, though somewhat inconclusive, marked the arrival of Octavian as a great force, despite his youth.

46   Philippi: Macedonian city founded by Philip II. It fell under Roman control in the 2nd century BC, and in October, 42 BC, provided the

site for a battle between the forces of Octavian and Mark Antony on the one side and those of Marcus Junius Brutus and Gaius Cassius Longinus, republican partisans and the two surviving assassins of Julius Caesar. Octavian and Antony won.

55 Callimachus: Greek poet (*ca.* 310-240 BC), born in Cyrene, Libya, and scholar at the Library of Alexandria. He was famous for his 120-volume bibliography of the Library.

56 Phlegra: in reality a peninsula in Macedonia, but in legend the site of Zeus' overthrow of the Giants.

58 Julian: the heirs of Julius; the Caesars.

81 Melian's hurt: after the Battle of Melos, in which the Melians were defeated by Athenian forces, all men fit enough to carry arms were killed and all the 77 women and children enslaved. Another version of the translation has this as "Lemnian's hurt".

81 Machaon: the son of Asclepius, famed as a surgeon and doctor (thus carrying on the family interest in this area), he also led an army in the Trojan War on the Greek side.

83 Chiron: a centaur, son of the Titan Kronos, and half-brother to Zeus, foster-son of Apollo, and sometime teacher of Achilles. His mother was the nymph, Philyra, who was making love to Kronos when the latter's wife suddenly appeared; in order to escape notice he transformed himself into a horse, and in this way sired a half-equine son. Chiron cured Phoenix, after he had been blinded by his father.

Androgeon, a wrestler and son of Minos who was killed by the Athenian king, Aegeus. The pollution that resulted from his death caused a plague, which could only be abated by an annual Athenian tribute of seven boys and seven girls to be devoured by the Minotaur, a half-bull, half-human creature kept in the palace at Knossos.

Tantalus: (Tantalos), a character from the Greek myths, most famous for his eternal punishment in Tartarus, by which he was made to stand in a pool of water beneath a fruit tree with low branches, with the fruit always eluding his grasp, and the water always receding before he could take a drink. Origin of the word "tantalise".

IMITATED FROM PROPERTIUS: Lib:3, Eleg:5, p.127

[Translation made 1738.]

6 Castalia: site of a Spring sacred to the Muses on Mt Helicon.

8 Aganippe: another spring on Helicon, and also the name of the naiad (water-nymph) associated with it.

12 Bacchus: god of wine and revels.

35 Pindus: (Pindos), a mountain range in northern Greece.

39 seven sisters: the Pleiades, nymph-companions of Artemis and daughters of the Titan, Atlas. Nurses and teachers of Bacchus.

40 Bootes: (*also sp.* Boötes), according to legend, the inventor of the plough; an ox-herder. The wagon is his ox-cart. (This also refers to the constellation, the Big Dipper.)

46 Alecto: one of the Furies. in the Aeneid, Juno demanded of Alecto not to permit the Trojans (ancestors of the modern Romans, according to Virgil), to have their way with King Latinus or to besiege Italian cities.

47 Tityus: one of the Giants, son of Zeus and Elara. The latter was hidden in the earth by her consort but her son grew too large for her womb and he was carried to term by Gaia, the earth-goddess. When an adult, he tried to rape Leto, daughter of two other Titans, at Hera's command, but was killed by Artemis and Apollo.

48 triple dog: the three-headed dog, Cerberus, which guarded the gates of Hades.

50 Ixion: king of the Lapiths, a Hellenic tribe in Thessaly. When he married he promised a significant bride-price; when he failed to deliver, his father-in-law, Deionius stole some of Ixion's horses. Ixion invited his father-in-law to a feast at Larissa, but when the guest arrived, Ixion pushed him into a bed of burning coals, causing his death. He was said to be the first Greek to have killed a member of his own family, as well as having transgressed traditional guest-host etiquette. Ixion later went mad and was shunned by all his neighbours.

58 Crassus: Marcus Linnius Crassus (*ca* 115-53 BC), Roman general who served under Sulla, then made a fortune from property speculation, served as Consul with Pompey after putting down the slave revolt led by Spartacus, and finally acted as patron of Julius Caesar, with whom he and Pompey acted as the unofficial First Triumvirate. His successful career came to an end while he was governor of Syria, when he invaded Parthia; this decision was fatal: his armies were crushed and he lost his life at the Battle of Carrhae. Carrhae is modern Harran, in Turkey, close to the Syrian border.

Lightning Source UK Ltd.
Milton Keynes UK
UKHW012112121121
393874UK00002B/655